ARISE

Jungian Insights for the Christian Journey

Rev. Msgr. Chester P. Michael, S.T.D.

INFINITY
PUBLISHING

ISBN 0-7414-6974-X Paperback
ISBN 0-7414-6975-8 eBook
Library of Congress Control Number: 2011941234

Printed in the United States of America

Published March 2012

INFINITY PUBLISHING
1094 New DeHaven Street, Suite 100
West Conshohocken, PA 19428-2713
Toll-free (877) BUY BOOK
Local Phone (610) 941-9999
Fax (610) 941-9959
Info@buybooksontheweb.com
www.buybooksontheweb.com

Grateful acknowledgement is also made to the Association of Friends of Teilhard de Chardin and to Thomas Coffey of Dimension Books for permission to use the excerpt at the end of Chapter One from Teilhard de Chardin: *Building the Earth*. Copyright 1965 by Dimension Books, Inc., Denville, N.J.

i

This book, originally titled <u>Arise: A Christian Psychology of Love</u>, was first published in 1981 by Monsignor Chester P. Michael's non-profit organization, *The Open Door, Inc.* In 2010 Monsignor Michael and the Board of Directors made a decision to use a publisher's services to mass-market the book. The book you hold in your hands is the result of that decision. Many have benefitted from Monsignor Michael's work through *The Open Door, Inc.*, most especially the attendees of his retreats, and students of *The Spiritual Direction Institute* (SDI) in Charlottesville, Virginia. The *Spiritual Direction Institute* is a two-year program which began in 1989 and continues today to enrich the lives of seekers. Monthly sessions and four week-long retreats offer a venue and a supportive environment for spiritual development within the Catholic Christian tradition. Enrollment is open to all.

This book provides insights into our sexuality, the polarities of our human condition, the need for discipline in daily living, the role of the unconscious in the development of spirituality, and an appreciation of the expansive love of God for each of us to develop the unique potential within. The splendor of God is mirrored in each of us. Monsignor Michael's challenging insights which originate from Jungian psychology illuminate the possibilities for faithfully developing our human potential to the glory of God.

Inquiries concerning SDI and retreats should be sent to The Open Door Inc., P.O. Box 855, Charlottesville, VA 22902 or to Al Mirmelstein at amirmelstein@nlrg.com or Patty Huffman at palhuffman@yahoo.com.

In Memoriam

Marie Louise Daly
Friend, Counselee, Benefactor

+ March 14, 1981

TABLE OF CONTENTS

INTRODUCTION

The central idea of this book is that the key to a successful, happy life is the fullest possible development of our unlimited potential for love.

The love of which we speak goes beyond mere affection, desire, or passion. There are many kinds of love, depending on the object of our love—God, our neighbor, the world, and ourselves. Real love, however, is always the result of a free decision by a rational being who makes a commitment to the service of another, or others, predicated not on personal attachment alone but on a feeling of respect, sympathetic understanding, solicitude, and a willingness to sacrifice something of oneself for the good of the other.

At one time or another in our life we will have given or received parental, brotherly, or spousal love. To understand real love we need to recall the examples of mutual, unselfish love that we have experienced or observed. The prime example of love is the relationship that existed between Jesus Christ and his Heavenly Father as seen in the four Gospel accounts in the Bible. The life of Jesus also vividly exemplified the extremes to which true love is willing to go for the sake of the beloved—namely, suffering and death. To understand the mystery of love, we must study and reflect upon how much God loves us, how much Jesus loved his Heavenly Father, and how much Jesus loves us.

To develop our unlimited potential for love.

1

Much of our energy for love often remains untapped. What is worse, sometimes the human energy used for loving is misdirected and becomes an instrument of violence and hatred. There are a number of reasons why we never actualize our full capability for love. This book attempts to discuss some of them and to suggest ways and means to encourage the release of more human energy in the positive direction of love rather than in the negative direction of antagonistic, disruptive, destructive action.

Modern depth psychology has uncovered mankind's immense powers for growth in love and maturity. Having discovered and somewhat clarified the laws and means by which love operates within human life, mankind now has the responsibility to actualize more fully the human potential for love. This obligation is all the greater when we realize that when the human energies for love are used improperly, the likelihood is that they will be used to attain the opposite of the goals of love. Instead of taking us more speedily toward our proper destiny of unity, they will, if neglected, lead us farther away from our goal.

A mature person may be defined as one who has fully actualized his or her capabilities for love and has directed these energies toward the right goals and with the right priorities. Among Christians this is also the meaning of a saint, except that in sanctity special emphasis is given to an explicit and unlimited love of God. For example, prayer occupies a considerable portion of the time and energy of a saint's life on earth. Whereas the secular spends most of his or her time relating to others. Maturity, sanctity, wholeness—all refer to that situation in life where all of our energies for love have been released and directed with the right priority toward the greatest possible development of one's true inner self, toward other human beings, and toward God.

Several assumptions concerning love, for which no attempt will be made to give extensive proof, are made in this book. To do so would considerably lengthen the book and lead us astray from the basic purpose of this book: namely, to instruct and encourage people in some of the ways to release and direct their energies of love toward sanctity and maturity. The basic assumption is that the goal and destiny of all existence is a unity through love. Our premise is that the only way for human beings to attain lasting happiness and fulfillment is to devote all their energies toward the unification of all reality in an experience of true love. Such an experience of love is what the Bible calls God (Cf. I John 4:16). As Christians, we believe and assume that such unity will be accomplished only through the risen Christ. "When finally, all has been subjected to the Son, he will then subject himself to the One who made all things subject to him, so that God may be all in all" (I Cor. 15:28).

Another presupposition of this book is the verity of the statement made in the First Epistle of John: "God is love and he who abides in love abides in God and God in him" (I John 4:16). Therefore, to separate love and religion is impossible; and if we are to discuss intelligently the topic of love, either explicitly or implicitly we must bring God into the discussion. It naturally follows that this book will be a book on religious values; particularly it will be a book for Christian believers who accept Jesus Christ as the manifestation of God upon earth.

Having made these assumptions, we shall attempt to show the value and need for Christians to make full use of the psychological tools which scientific research has given to our generation. The tools that will be used in this book come for the most part from Carl Gustav Jung and his disciples. Acknowledgement and thanks must be given to Father Josef Goldbrunner to whom we owe our first introduction and interpretation of Jung. Jungian psychology has identified and classified many of the immense powers hidden in the unconscious depths of human nature. Thanks to Jung's insights we are now able to actualize more easily the vast psychic energies of love present in every human soul.

CHAPTER ONE

THE CHALLENGE OF OUR TIMES

The need for unselfish, other-directed love is greater today than perhaps in any previous period of human history. Either we intensify and broaden our practice of true, generous love or we perish. The enemies of love in today's world are powerful, extensive, and dangerous. As we discover and unleash new energies, new knowledge, new technology, new and faster means of communication, these same powers can be used to do harm as well as to do good. Violence, discrimination, greed, injustice have great capabilities to create disunity, hatred, insecurity and fear. They can bring about the total alienation of mankind and a Sartrian hell on earth. Nevertheless, increased knowledge and new energies are also available for the intensification of love. This then is the challenge of our times: to use all the new scientific discoveries in the service of love rather than in the service of hate, to foster unity rather than disunity.

Scientific research has developed a variety of methods and means that could be used to facilitate the work of the unification of mankind and creation; but science and technology are incapable of producing the unselfish love and motivation required to use properly these new tools. Love is in a category of reality over which science has neither the control nor the knowledge nor the ability to handle. Love is a spiritual force not subject to the laws of

4

Does social media show e que love or hinder it?

scientific technology. Science can only develop efficient machines and tools which human beings may use either for carrying out their destiny of love or for hindering it.

In recent generations we have witnessed a tremendous surge toward the unification of the earth. World-wide communication by highly developed media makes for simultaneous knowledge of events in every part of the globe. Jet air travel draws the population of the world closer each year. As society advances step by step toward one world, the demand for a high degree of maturity on the part of everyone becomes greater. Only a world population willing to pay the price of mature, unselfish love and service toward others is capable of using the tools of modern society for the greatest good of humanity. The longer we neglect to do this, the more these tools will be used for violence and destruction.

In the providence of God there are certain periods of history when the rate of progress in knowledge, energy, and power is much faster than others. Our present age is a period of more rapid development than perhaps any previous age of history. The world has moved ahead at a fantastic rate of speed in almost every phase of human progress. The actual knowledge that modern man possesses has doubled again and again. A study of the history of evolution indicates that there have been other critical periods of tension along the upward path of humanity from a more simple to a more complex state of existence. As the time drew near for a lower form to evolve into a higher being, the lower state experienced a tremendous build-up of pressure. Then somewhere in the world, this tension finally brought about an eruption into a higher and more complicated form of being. Once the new level was attained, all the forces of energy rushed to this point and concentrated their efforts upon the perfection of the new species that had just evolved. Here the tension again built up until a new cycle of evolution was ready to burst forth.

With the advent of humankind, the evolutionary powers of God have been at work perfecting human nature. These forces within humanity have as their immediate goal to bring us to a higher state of consciousness and spiritual maturity. The ultimate goal is a unity of love with God himself. This objective can be attained only by the release into our conscious life of all those vast stores of psychic energy which are now hidden in our unconscious inner being. These spiritual energies rising from the unconscious should be directed primarily to perfecting our capacity for love. Because we are free, the perfection of our love must await the freely given cooperation of mankind. With our free will we must choose to work to bring about the perfection of the human race and the unification of all creation in God. This is the awesome challenge given to the men of every generation but especially to us who have so much more knowledge and power at our disposal than our predecessors ever dreamed possible.

Will the people of our generation experience a new surge of growth in maturity and love, or will we suffer some terrible tragedy and setback? A study of past history reveals other times when the future looked as promising or as threatening as it does today. Sometimes the people of other generations accepted the challenge of their era and the world experienced a new growth toward unity. An example of one such time is the first centuries after the death and resurrection of Jesus. On the other hand, we know of periods of history when the people failed to read the signs of the times or refused to cooperate with the opportunities given to them for growth. The result was another tragic fall of mankind and a regression to a lower level of existence. Examples of this would be the collapse of the cultures of the Greeks and Egyptians during the centuries before the Christian era. We should profit from the examples of the past and not allow a similar tragedy to happen to us. With the help of God we can, and must, triumph over our mediocrity, our sloth, our pride, our greed, our lust for power and pleasure. We have God's assurance, repeated many times in the Bible, that God and love will, in the end, triumph upon earth. (Cf. Rev. 21:1-7; Romans 8:18-39; I Cor. 15:20-28; Eph. 2:4-10; Phil. 3:12-21). We must dedicate the energies of our whole being to the full maturation of our abilities to love. God will be with us to help us, but we are free to refuse or to cooperate with God's grace.

The practice of pure, unselfish love requires a high degree of self-discipline. We must either learn to develop our faculties for love to a much higher degree than is being done at present or we may witness the collapse and destruction of our world. Both centripetal and centrifugal forces are at work in today's society. At the moment it seems a toss-up as to which will win possession of the world. Every day we see and hear in our newspapers and on the TV screen abundant evidence of the centrifugal forces of war, violence, disunity. What are we doing to foster the centripetal force of love which can bind us together and unite the people of the world?

We hear much talk about love today. It seems that a wide variety of persons have received new insights into the purpose and value of love. However, there is much confusion and uncertainty about the true meaning of love and the knowledge and training necessary for the development of its energies. What is the place of religion in fostering human love? What can psychology contribute to our understanding and intensification of love? What do philosophers have to contribute to our knowledge and practice of love? How can we bring together the many disciplines which show interest and understanding in the value and importance of love?

To develop fully our capacities for love, there are three distinct spheres in which we need to exert ourselves. The first of these is our conscious life which must be adequately trained and developed. This will require the disciplining and perfecting of our intellect will, memory, emotions, senses, and imagination and will also require the strengthening of our bodily health to enable us to carry out the physical parts of the tasks entrusted to us. Secondly, we need to go down into the depths of our inner being to uncover and lead forth into consciousness the powers of our unconscious which will decide ultimately the direction our life will take. Thirdly, we must develop our sense of community—our ability to relate to others—in order to unite our energies with others to work together for the progress of love and unity and the maturation of the human race. As far as possible we should be working in all three of these spheres; however, at different times in our life one area will need more emphasis than another.

The lives of nations and civilizations, as well as the lives of individuals, reach certain points of decision or forks in the road where a choice has to be made. These points of decision are called crises and the word *kairos* is used in the New Testament for the special time given to an individual or a group of people to make the decision in this time of crisis. Thinking people all over the world are claiming that this present time is such a *kairos*. In the past, civilizations such as Israel, Egypt, Babylonia, Greece and Rome have found themselves at such crossroads of history. For at least some of these cultures, we have documentary proof that certain prophets were able to read the signs of the times and warn the people of the imminent collapse of their world unless a drastic change of direction was made. In most instances the people failed to heed the warnings of the prophets and the collapse that had been foretold occurred.

As Christians we believe that with the coming of Jesus, the people of the world have been given new helps to enable them to rise above their selfishness and make a decision for God, for love. At the very beginning of the Christian era, Christian love challenged the might of the Roman Empire and won a victory for love. Again and again during the past twenty centuries Christian love has challenged the forces of hatred and evil. Sometimes we have won, at other times the battle has been lost. Today, the challenge to our charity is as great or greater than any other time since the first century of Christianity.

"Mankind still shows signs of a reserve, a formidable potential…of progress. Think of the immensity of the powers, ideas, and persons not discovered or harnessed or born or synthesized. In terms of "energy"…the human race is still very young and fresh. The earth is still far from having completed its sidereal evolution. True, we can imagine all sorts of catastrophes which might intervene to cut short this great development. But for 300 million years now, Life has been going on paradoxically in the midst of improbability. Does that not indicate that it is marching forward, sustained by some complicity in the motive forces of the Universe? The real difficulty…is…how this progress can go on for a long time yet at its present rate, without life exploding of itself or blowing up the earth on which it was born…Progress, if it is to continue, will not happen by itself…What steps must we take in relation to this forward march? I see two…a great hope, in common…A passionate love of growth, of being, that is what we need. Down with the cowards and sceptics, the pessimists and the unhappy, the weary and the stagnant…There is only one way which leads upwards; the one which, through greater organization, leads to greater synthesis and unity. Here again, then, down with the pure individualists, the egoist, who expect to grow by excluding or diminishing their brothers—individually, nationally, or racially…The future of the earth is in our hands. How shall we decide?…It is not our heads or our bodies which we must bring together, but our hearts."

(Pierre Teilhard de Chardin, *Building the Earth*, pp. 104-111)

CHAPTER TWO

A PERSONAL CHALLENGE

Each of us should feel a personal challenge to do all we can to meet the needs of the times. No matter how small I feel myself to be, I am called by God to do something worthwhile to help the world attain the fullness destined for it. Regardless of my education or lack of education, regardless of the specialization of my past training or my present situation, I always can make a worthwhile contribution to the total growth of our world.

In a certain limited sense the world is less perfect today because I have failed to do my part in the past. If I had been more loving, more unselfish, the world would be better. What I have done in the past, what I do now, and what I will do in the future influences mankind for better or worse. For those who have no direct contact with me, my influence may be slight; but it is present. Only God knows whether my neglected virtues would have been the bit of influence that could have changed others' lives from bad to good. Certainly, my influence for good or for ill is greatest upon those people with whom I associate in my daily life. I owe to them, as well as to God and myself, the very best efforts I can give to the perfecting of the talents entrusted to me.

Instead of sitting back and blaming others for the ills of our modern world, I must assume a personal responsibility for doing all I can to change the world for the better. As long as I continue to blame others for the troubles around me, I can feel comfortable in my mediocrity and selfish pursuits. I will do something worthwhile only when I face the fact that as a citizen of today's world I am at least partly responsible for the world as it now exists. As a member of the human race, I must be willing to shoulder some of the burden of the past and present sins of the world. Having been called to be a disciple of Christ, I must become the redeemer of my brethren, not to the same degree as Jesus Christ, but to the utmost extent of my capabilities.

Like Christ, I should freely choose to take up the cross of my brothers' sufferings and give my life for their redemption. I am not asked to do the impossible but only to carry what I can. With St. Paul, I should be able to say, "I am happy to suffer for you as I am now suffering, because it gives me a chance to complete in my own person something of the untold pains which Christ suffered on behalf of his body, the Church" (Col. 1:24).

Apart from the influence my external behavior has on my brethren, the particular maturity of my inner being also influences others. The pulsations of my unconscious and interior attitudes extend out over the world like ripples from a stone dropped in the middle of a lake. The bonds that unite the human race extend from me until the whole world is enveloped. Regardless of whether or not I realize it and intend it, by the very fact of being alive and existing, I exert an influence for better or worse upon others.

Never must I allow myself to make the mistake of imagining that I am unimportant or that what I do has little or no effect upon others. Every human being is important in the work of the redemption of the world. Others may be more important, but I have a definite place assigned to me by Almighty God. There is a niche that I am expected to fill; and, if I fail to accomplish my particular task, a certain part of the fabric of the world's perfection will be lost. I am needed; others depend upon me; and they will not be able to do a good job in their vocation unless I do a good job in mine. I must work in all three spheres of life: (1) the external world of mankind; (2) the world of my own intellect, will and conscious faculties; (3) the inner world of my unconscious psyche of repressed and undeveloped desires and ideas. All are important; but the area where I will do the most good for God and others is down deep in my heart where the basic attitudes which govern my exterior conduct and influence others are formed.

In the outer world, my efforts are frequently thwarted by a lack of cooperation from others or by causes beyond my control. It is only in my inner world that I am able to be truly the master of my destiny. People may imprison me or hamper me so that I have no external freedom to do apparent good. However, no one can enter my soul-castle and destroy my inner freedom unless I open the door and allow him to enter. Even God himself respects the privacy of the inner chambers of my soul. This is the real meaning of freedom: I am truly responsible for the conduct of my inner life. If I so choose, I can cut off my inner world from God, from my brethren, and even from my own final goal in life. The result will be that terrible loneliness we call "hell". On the other hand, if I so choose, I can open my heart and soul to God, to my brethren and to the responsibilities I have to them. The result will be a beautiful growth of my own soul and a profound influence for good upon others.

In the microcosm of my inner heart, the whole outer world lives. Without spending too much time worrying about what others are doing to help or harm the world, I should convert this inner world of mine into the likeness of Jesus Christ. First of all, I should experience a certain dissatisfaction with my present state and a desire to alter it. Rather than allow myself to grow comfortable in my mediocrity, I need to take time to see my lack of wholeness (completeness). When I see all the work to be done in my own being, I will be spared the temptation of imagining that I have already done enough. No matter how much I might have accomplished in the past, there is more to be done. On the other hand, I must not be discouraged and overwhelmed by the seemingly gigantic size of the tasks facing me. "I can do all things in him who strengthens me" (Phil. 4:13).

The conversion of my inner heart is primarily a matter of transforming my attitudes toward God, myself, my brethren, and the outside physical world. I must try to see persons and things as God sees them. I can do this if I meditate frequently upon Jesus Christ and learn from his words and actions what attitudes of mine need to be changed or developed. I must understand where I have been guilty of the worship of alien gods: the false gods of pleasure, money, power, and pride. I must try to discover what steps to take to bring myself and the rest of mankind from where we are now to where we should be.

Besides this knowledge, I must desire the highest possible wholeness for myself and others. No one can attain maturity without intense desires for wholeness and perfection. My desire to grow in maturity must be so deep and great that I am willing to pay any price, no matter how high, to attain it. My desires, also, should persist throughout my life, regardless of how often I fail or make mistakes. It is possible to start late in life and reach our goal; but the later we start, the greater desire and more effort we need. However, I must not be discouraged by my past failures; with the help of God's grace I can be forgiven and start anew.

If my thirst for wholeness and perfection is truly deep and great, I will rise after each fall and persist in the long struggle for holiness. On the other hand, the more whole I am, the easier I will tolerate the frustration of some of my ambitions and dreams. Instead of beating hopelessly and desperately against the walls and blind alleys into which I wander, I must be willing to face temporary defeat, admit my mistake, and then turn back to find a new and better path to the perfection destined for me. There must be no despair, no cessation of effort, no attempt to escape from the humiliation of failures. Failure and defeat are part of the normal human's life; I must face them and look for new ways to progress.

Besides knowledge and desire, I must make a total commitment of my life and energy to the pursuit of wholeness. God never asks the impossible, but he does ask that I cooperate with him to the best of my ability. The more generous my cooperation, the better chance I have of attaining my goal. God's mercy is so great that there is always hope for me as long as I take whatever energy and equipment I now possess and do all I can to gain other talents and use them to the best possible advantage. In addition, I must be humble enough to seek help from others who can assist me in becoming better.

Regardless of my limitations or past failures, I can trust in God to give me what I lack in order to attain my destiny in life. God knows all things, he knows what is best on every given occasion. God is also all-powerful, all-good, all-just and takes into consideration all my weaknesses and limitations. Finally, God is all-loving and all-merciful; he has loved me enough to be humiliated and to die upon a cross for me. If I meditate sufficiently on these facts, I should be able to attain the loving trust which God asks of me. Despite his many sins, David trusted in God's help. As a result, God took good care of David, while those in the desert died in their sin when they failed to trust in God's help (Psalm 77).

In no way do I contradict my faith and trust in God if I make use of every possible means to grow in natural maturity. God wants me to perfect my nature as highly as possible. When I use my natural talents to grow in wholeness, I show a seriousness of purpose and generosity in my commitment to God and God's goal for me. The more balanced is my human nature, the more easily and quickly I can grow in the Christian life of grace and union of love with God and others. The more I grow in natural perfection, the more easily will the grace of Christ's life, death, and resurrection penetrate and sanctify my whole being. By my efforts to cooperate with God's will in the perfection of my

14

outer and inner being, I become truly the master of my destiny.

St. Ignatius of Loyola has beautifully described the generosity that one must show in responding to God's call to wholeness: "To give and not to count the cost, to fight and not to heed the wounds, to toil and not to seek for rest, to labor and not to ask for reward." This total dedication to love will show itself in the efforts I make to attain as complete a mastery over myself as is possible. Through daily self-denial and a sacrifice of egotism, I learn to control my conscious and unconscious faculties. I need this self-possession to make a total gift of my being and life in love to God and others. This self-control which is essential to my spiritual growth will be attained only by constant discipline. One by one, I must uncover my talents, energies, and the powers of my inner world. These great forces must be brought to the surface of consciousness, trained, and put to work for the good of everyone—God, mankind, my own maturity, and the perfection of the physical universe.

In this work of conversion and growth, I must be careful to keep order and balance. Wholeness is not found in disorder but in a tranquility of order where there is a place for everything and everything is in its place. This does not mean an absence of conflict and struggle but rather an absence of anarchy and rebellion. I must find a way to grow in the particular environment in which I find myself. Many changes will be made before I reach the goal of unity and love, but they should be orderly changes and motivated by the all-consuming desire to attain a higher order and balance than my present one. As long as I live, I must not become satisfied or content with my present state of affairs. Always my motto must be "Excelsior." I must strive to climb ever higher and higher toward the distant and lofty peak of maturity, love, community, and unity.

CHAPTER THREE

THE LAW OF POLARITY: OPPOSITES ATTRACT

A law of polarity seems to be at work throughout all reality: wherever we find the proper order, all creation is arranged with opposite poles. In physical, psychological, and spiritual areas we find this law of polarity producing new energy and accomplishing great good for the benefit of all. Among living plants and animals the two poles are called the masculine and feminine. In some mysterious way the interaction and synthesis of the two poles seem to carry on the work of creation in nonliving matter as well as in living beings. In matter the most obvious example of this is the sphere of the earth which revolves around a central axis with the two poles at the end of this axis. As the earth rotates, a tremendous field of magnetic energy is created at each extremity. A similar creation of magnetic energy can be brought about in a piece of iron when its molecules are arranged in an orderly fashion facing opposite poles. There is a great mystery about this magnetic power; we know that the attraction between the two poles is productive of energy even though we do not know exactly why this is true.

The interaction of the positive and negative poles in electricity brings about a similar display of electrical energy that fills our modern world. The principle of polarity is at work in every light bulb, every electric motor, or electric appliance which we use. In every chemical reaction the tension or polarity between two or more chemical elements produces a synthesis of the original elements to form something entirely new. Water, for example, is a balance of tension between oxygen and hydrogen. As long as the balance is maintained, we are able to enjoy the new thing that has been produced.

If the two poles are allowed to follow the attraction they feel for each other and come together, there will be a transfer of energy from one to the other that is productive of a new reality. The two opposites converge into a synthesis that produces new life and increases the energy and activity of the two original participants in the union. The two poles having opposite tendencies merge in a union that is more alive, richer and fuller than either or both of the parties had when existing alone. During the time of union a certain tension must be maintained. As long as this balance is maintained, a constant pulsation of energy will be transferred from pole to pole. If one or the other pole is eliminated, a situation of stasis occurs whereby all life and energy, all enthusiasm and spontaneity come to a halt.

Polarity is necessary for the origin of all life, growth, power, and creativity. In order for the fusion between the two poles to be productive, there will be a pressure or stress between the two extremes. This tension between the poles is not always easy to bear; yet it is necessary to arouse and activate the sleeping potential of any being. As long as the correct balance can be maintained between the two opposites, the union remains effective and capable of creating new energy. A proper synthesis adds the new element of community (union) without destroying the individuality of the original poles.

The key to the successful use of the law of polarity seems to be the ability to maintain both balance and tension without destroying either of the poles. We speak of "tension capacity" and mean the ability of either an inanimate object or a living being to withstand stress and strain. The higher the tension capacity, the more productive the synthesis will be. A person or an object with a low tension capacity may be injured or destroyed if subjected to too much stress. Therefore such persons and things need to be protected from undue strain. No matter how low the tension capacity of these participants might be, it needs to be brought into balance with a proportionate opposing force; otherwise, it will become sterile and useless. If we are to grow in maturity and reach the wholeness for which we are destined, it is essential that we develop our tension capacity to as high a degree as possible.

In the field of personality and character growth too, the law of polarity is constantly at work. For example, a balance must be found between the conscious and unconscious, between the individual and the community, between masculinity and femininity. Every attribute exists in a state of tension and balance with an opposite characteristic in our personality. The greater the tension that can be tolerated between these qualities, the more creative and productive it will be. If the tension is dissolved by favoring one virtue and denying the other, the inter-play is lost and growth ceases. Even the value which was favored becomes lifeless and sterile. Therefore, faith in God needs to stand in the proper balance with faith in oneself; love of self must be allowed to exist in tension with love of others. The well-balanced, mature personality will be able to handle both freedom and submission, independence and dependence. The mature person will know when to be an introvert and when to be an extravert; furthermore one must keep a balance between the physical and spiritual; the intellect and feeling; sensation and intuition; knowledge and love; orderliness and spontaneity. We must be choleric and melancholic; sanguine and phlegmatic; full of self-confidence yet fully confident in God, courageous but prudent.

When we speak of wholeness and integrity in a person, we refer to the unity which results from a harmonious balance of all the potentials one possesses. If the proper order is present in a personality, the diverse qualities will be symmetrically arranged at opposite poles to other qualities which are equally as good. Through the interaction or dialogue between these attributes, a person grows in wholeness. If the tension capacity of a person is strong, many encounters between these opposing forces are possible and new growth and tremendous energies of life are released for the benefit of the person involved and others who come in contact with him. For example, justice must be tempered with charity, regardless of how difficult it might be to reconcile them. It is by the interplay between these opposing duties of charity and justice that we grow in maturity and fulfill the obligations of our state in life. The same polarity must be kept between the other tensions in our life: God and man, individual and community, authority and obedience, courage and prudence, head and heart.

We may define evil or sin as a disorder: that is, a lack of proper balance between opposing virtues, or the absence of one or the other of these polarities. In human beings the disorder of sin often results from an unwillingness to endure the necessary tension. Many times the reason for avoiding or dissolving the tension is not so much unwillingness as the inability to endure the resulting stress of conflicting forces; and this cannot be called sin because it is not deliberately willed; but it will have tragic results. Our Christian faith and experience suggest to us that many of these non-sinful tragedies can be traced to the sinful neglect of some person in the past who deliberately failed to pay the necessary price of self-discipline to attain maturity. The low tension capacity that many of us now have is at least partly due to the sins of our ancestors who chose mediocrity, compromise, or escape from responsibility rather than undertake the necessary heroic struggle of the tensions in their lives. A deliberate refusal by us today to endure the strain resulting from the polarities in our life can have evil and disastrous consequences for future generations.

Regardless of the sins and failures of our forefathers, the responsibility of each new generation is to do all in its power to reverse the flight from tension and suffering. It is our task to build up our tension capacity, stand our ground, and face the stresses which confront us. Rather than run away from the hard work and struggle involved in finding and keeping the proper balance between opposing forces, we must use every possible means to keep alive the polarities of creativity and growth. We must learn how to resolve and reconcile the strain and conflict without destroying the power or losing the energy that results from the fusion of the two poles. Throughout the years of our life, our responsibility for growth in maturity requires us to face each new tension, bring about a successful encounter between the opposites, and then integrate the resulting increase of energy into our personality.

There are two areas of tension above all others in which the right balance must be found if we wish to attain the wholeness of maturity: the balance between God's grace and our cooperation, and the tension and balance that should exist between the conscious and unconscious areas of our being. In the life of Jesus Christ we see these two tensions beautifully resolved along with an even higher tension—the tension between his divine and human natures. To resolve and maintain a proper balance in our tensions we must return again and again to reflection on the life of Jesus Christ.

Divine Grace and Human Effort

Ever since the fifth century of the Christian era, theologians have discussed the relationship of divine grace and human effort. The most famous of the controversies over this question was that between St. Augustine and Pelagius. Pelagius maintained the natural goodness of human nature and the need to exert our human will and other natural powers to grow in virtue. Augustine insisted our human nature was corrupted by original sin and that it was impossible to advance in virtue by our natural powers without God's additional help. This supplemental aid was called "actual grace". The main text upon which Augustine relied for this teaching was Phillipians 2:13. "It is God who works in you both to will and accomplish the good you do." Augustine's theory was adopted by the Church; Pelagius' teaching (Pelagianism) was declared heretical.

Today theologians are inclined to downplay the antithesis between nature and grace, the natural and supernatural. God is seen as the author of both our natural endowments as well as those of special helps called "actual graces". No longer is human nature seen as corrupt but rather as weakened by the inherited effects of the sins of our ancestors and our own sins. Despite the countless words already written about the relationship between nature and grace and our growth in holiness and maturity, the mystery of human freedom and God's ever-present providence remains. With Augustine we fully agree that we are totally dependent on God's help for the good we accomplish. We cannot even want to be good unless God gives us the desire to do so. In response to St. Paul's question: "What have you that you have not received?" (I Cor. 4:7), we readily reply, "Nothing." Nevertheless we are ready to admit with Pelagius the need for human cooperation in growth in virtue and holiness. If the concept of human freedom has any validity, it means that we are capable of placing obstacles to our progress in maturity and sanctity.

A close study of both the Old and New Testaments will reveal the paradoxical insistence upon dependence on God and the need of human efforts to cooperate with God in attaining salvation. Constant scriptural insistence upon prayer clearly indicates our need of God. "Ask and you will receive. Seek and you will find. Knock and it will be opened to you. For the one who asks, receives. The one who seeks, finds. The one who knocks, enters" (Matt. 7:7-9). Yet, two verses later in the same chapter, Jesus urges us to "strive to enter the narrow gate…How narrow is the gate that leads to life, how rough the road, and how few there are who find it" (Matt. 7:13-14).

How the two elements of human effort and divine grace blend is still a mystery. Both must be present like opposite poles for any bonafide growth in maturity and holiness. Somehow human virtue is a blending of the two. If we consider God's help and human freedom as the two opposite poles, the interaction of these two poles is required to produce authentic human growth. We know that God wants us to actualize our full potential for love. "God wants everyone to be saved and reach a full knowledge of the truth" (Tim. 2:4). Therefore, we can be sure that God's grace and cooperation will never be lacking for our growth in wholeness. Apparently the only uncertainty is our own cooperation. Frequently, the reason we don't cooperate is not malice or human cantankerousness. Often it is due to ignorance, fear, lack of good experiences of love in the past, or other factors beyond our immediate control. The purpose of this book is to facilitate the removal of these obstacles to growth and encourage us to actualize the full potential of our ability to love.

Ideally nature and grace should exist together in a beautiful harmony within each person. However, very holy people, even canonized saints, are sometimes emotionally immature. Through no fault of their own, perhaps because of traumatic experiences or a lack of love in their childhood, these people became adults with a warped, neurotic nature. But, when they do the best they can to use whatever powers of nature and grace at their disposal, God does not deny them the grace of sanctity. For this reason, regardless of the sins of our past life or the weaknesses we have inherited, none of us can consider our case hopeless. Instead of despairing of our present lack of sanctity or maturity and perhaps blaming others for our lack of wholeness, we should work with whatever tension capacity and strength we have. With God's special helps and our own best efforts we can hope to succeed in attaining a balance of nature and grace which will lead us to maturity. We can indeed expect suffering and struggle along the way, but with perseverance, a mature union of divine grace and human effort will ultimately be attained. The more we learn about nature and grace, the more we realize how beautifully they can work together. Natural maturity or wholeness is the perfect foundation for growth in grace; similarly any bonafide increase of grace-filled union with God results in a corresponding perfecting of our nature.

Conscious and Unconscious

Within our human nature, a balance that is very difficult to resolve and maintain is a proper tension between our conscious and unconscious life. During the first twenty-five years of life most of our efforts should be given to finding and maintaining a good balance and synthesis between the polarities in our conscious life: i.e., the proper balance of body and spirit, intellect and will, thinking and feeling, judging and perceiving, introversion and extroversion. Sometime after puberty the unconscious areas of our psyche need to be uncovered, studied, and brought into a synthesis and balance with our conscious life. Once our unconscious life-forces begin to manifest themselves, much of the work of maturation from then until the end of life should be directed to the perfecting of this balance between the conscious and the unconscious.

There are various theories proposed today concerning the content of the unconscious and even concerning the exact meaning of this term. The theory suggested and followed in this book is that developed by Carl Gustav Jung and his disciples. Both words "conscious" and "unconscious" may be used as either adjectives or nouns. When used as a noun, "conscious" refers to that part of our being of which we are fully aware and over which we have some control. It is that part of us that has been realized and actualized. When we speak of the human "unconscious," we refer to everything within our inner being of which we are not immediately aware. Not only does this include past experiences which we have forgotten, but also and more important, the whole, vast potential of psychic energy which has not as yet been developed. Insofar as they remain unactualized in our life, these unconscious energies are unavailable to us by direct experience.

Jung has posited two distinct parts of the human unconscious. All of those personal experiences of our past which we have repressed or forgotten he calls the "personal unconscious." In addition, each of us carries a vast storehouse of experiences of our ancestors all the way back to the very beginnings of creation. Jung discovered this treasure-house of psychic energies hidden within the unconscious depths of every human being. He gave it the name, "collective unconscious" and called its contents "archetypes." By this he meant those primordial images implanted on the *tabula rasa* of the human psyche through the repeated experiences of hundreds of generations of our ancestors. These past experiences are the origin of the inherited instincts and habits that are present in all living creatures, plants as well as animals. To these primordial images in human beings Jung gave the specific name, "archetypes." By this he meant the original models or prototypes around which are gathered all our human experiences. Some examples of archetypes are: mother, father, child, hero, king, priest, magician, wise person, giant, superman, war, peace, birth, death, marriage, love, worship, enemy, friend, brother, sister, etc. Within the depths of our unconscious each of us carries an ideal image of what the typical situations of human history should be like.

Down through the centuries poets, writers, dramatists, and others who were especially in touch with these unconscious archetypes have succeeded in giving form to them by means of stories, legends, myths, drama, musical ballads, fairy tales, epic poetry, mythology, and religious literature. Thus these archetypes have been clothed with flesh and have become the themes around which the whole of human history has been built. Jung writes: "There are as many archetypes as there are typical situations in life. Endless repetition has engraved these experiences into our psychic constitution, not in the form of images filled with content, but at first only as forms without content, representing merely the possibility of a certain type of perception and actions." (Collected Works, Vol. 9, I, p. 48.) They are like photographic negatives that must first be developed through our conscious experiences in order to become available and useful to us.

The task of maturity is concerned with recognizing these archetypes buried within our unconscious and bringing them into a conjunction with the events of our personal, conscious life. Jung calls this task "individuation." His choice of the word "individuation" was to emphasize that fact that for each one of us maturity is unique and somewhat different from that of another individual. The goal of the individuation is the synthesis of all the opposites present in our personality.

There are certain archetypes that are specifically concerned with growth in maturity and our capabilities for love. Examples are the roles in life we must play which Jung calls "masks" or "persona"; the unconscious "shadow" of our repressed faults; masculinity and femininity to which Jung gave the names "animus" and "anima." Each of these will be treated at some length in later chapters of this book. Jung also developed quite fully the idea of complexes, e.g. inferiority complex, mother complex, etc. A complex is an archetype around which have coalesced a number of repressed experiences from our personal unconscious which now color our feelings, actions, decisions, and even our perceptions of reality without our being consciously aware of the distortion. These complexes need to be resolved in order for us to have good personal relationships of love with others.

There are four basic archetypes which Jung insists must be brought into consciousness and kept in constant balance and tension with the ego, the center of our conscious life. They are: the "self," the center of our inner unconscious being; God; other individuals, especially those of the opposite sex; and the community. The task of individuation is to bring about a marriage or conjunction between the ego and each of these four archetypes. Jung has called these four tasks: (1) AUTHENTICITY OF THE EGO, i.e., a harmonious and honest relationship between the ego and the inner self; (2) SIGNIFICANCE, i.e., a balance tension between God and our ego whereby we discover our true destiny and significance in the total plan of God's creation; (3) TRANSPARENCY, i.e., the openness to other individuals; (4) SOLIDARITY, i.e., the experience of our oneness with the rest of the human race and even with the whole of creation.

The process of individuation is a spiral growth circling again and again around three distinct centers: our conscious ego, our inner self, and God, who is the center of the whole of reality. In order to attain maturity, our personal life history must reflect this ascending spiral around these three centers. The backward swirl of the spiral indicates the pause or rest before proceeding upward and forward to new growth and should not be considered a regression but rather a plateau. Any attempt to avoid the tension required to maintain the balance necessary for growth in wholeness results in suppression and a reversion to a more infantile, immature way of living. A lifelong struggle is necessary in order to reconcile the tensions in our life's experiences and bring about a harmonious marriage or conjunction of these opposites.

Jung was strongly influenced by Hegelian philosophy which requires a synthesis as the successful outcome of the tension between thesis and antithesis. He found this theme of the marriage or conjunction of opposites recurring again and again in the writings of the early Christian Gnostics and the alchemists of the Middle Ages. Jung saw this union of opposites as the source of all the creative energies in life and reality, including the reality of God. The interplay between opposites sparks our creative powers and brings them into existence; but always, the first step along the way of new growth in wholeness is to get in touch with the archetypes of the collective unconscious and then to enter into the necessary struggle to bring about a harmonious balance between the conscious and the unconscious.

Night dreams, waking dreams, and fantasies are some ways by which we can discover the contents of our unconscious. The unconscious speaks to us when we are asleep or at certain times when we are awake. However, the voice of the unconscious uses symbolic language which is often difficult for us to translate. Jung maintains that unless we succeed in correctly interpreting the voice of the unconscious and, at the right time of our life, apply ourselves to the conscious development and actualization of our unconscious potential, we can expect serious conflicts to arise between our conscious and unconscious. However, these conflicts are challenges calling us to dig deeper into our unconscious to uncover the potential for love and growth which is behind each complex. We must then develop this archetype in our conscious life and bring it into a good balance with the other facets of our personality.

Like the conflicts between nature and grace, the conflicts that arise between our conscious and unconscious life cannot be resolved by ignoring or denying the validity of one or the other. The unconscious forces must one by one be brought to the surface of our consciousness, faced boldly, and then brought into a proper balance and union with the contents of our conscious life. During our youth we are often unaware of the need of this synthesis because the unconscious is still asleep or because we have repressed and forgotten the conflicts of our early life. However, it is impossible and quite undesirable to keep these conflicts repressed all our life. Even if we were able to do so, the result would be a frustration of the unique destiny for which we have been created.

The task of reconciling the conscious and unconscious is never completed. We may reach certain levels of maturity where we are able momentarily to relax and feel that at least one tension is substantially under control; but new tasks will almost immediately demand our attention. We must be careful not to proceed too quickly or too slowly in our efforts to uncover our unconscious energies and bring them into balance with our already developed conscious powers.

There is a proper time in life for each new task. If we try to expose too soon the depths of our unconscious, the conflict between the conscious and unconscious may be so formidable that we either collapse under the strain or become so discouraged that henceforth we flee from the whole quest for maturity; on the other hand, if we delay too long the process of individuation we miss many opportunities to grow in maturity. It is best to proceed with slow, but deliberate, speed, facing the particular tasks each period of life presents. The tasks facing the eighteen year old are quite different from those facing a person of twenty-five years. Similarly, the challenges of life at twenty-eight are considerably different from those we face at thirty-five or forty-five. The tension is always between what we actually are and what we could be. Our competition should not be with others but between what we have already actualized of our talents and abilities and that vast, apparently unlimited potential for love, goodness, wholeness, which still lies buried within our unconscious. Again and again, at each particular stage of growth we need to delve into our unconscious, face the particular archetype awaiting actualization, and then set to work to bring it into conscious reality.

CHAPTER FOUR

STAGES OF GROWTH

If we are able to develop our unconscious potential for love to the highest possible maturity, new capabilities will be actualized at different periods of our lives. The more knowledge we can have of the different stages of growth which are normally experienced, the clearer picture we will have of the particular tasks that challenge us at different periods of life.

A variety of schemas has been suggested for identifying the stages of growth through which we must pass to attain the fullness of life. For example, some of the Hindus in India divide life into four ages: 0-25, education; 25-50, active life; 50-75, contemplative life of prayer; 75-death, age of wisdom. The schema which is proposed in this chapter was first suggested by Father Josef Goldbrunner, priest-psychologist of Munich, Germany, and is also based somewhat upon the psychology of Carl Gustav Jung. It proposes a division of life into three basic periods of twenty-eight years each, and each of these periods is divided into four stages of growth.

Physiologists maintain that every cell of our physical body undergoes a complete change of content approximately once every seven years, and many men and women testify that they have experienced some kind of psychological, emotional, intellectual, or spiritual change in their personality approximately every seven years. The existence of a crisis of growth each seven years is true of so many different people from such diverse backgrounds that it may be worth one's time and effort to check back over one's past life to see whether or not the same has been true. The change from one stage of growth to another does not necessarily fall during the exact year that is a multiple of seven; but if you give yourself a leeway of a year or two in either direction, you will find it fascinating to check in your own memory the following years of life: 7—14—21—28—35—42—49—56—63—70—77—84.

One should test these suggestions with his or her own life's experiences to see how far they conform to one's situation. There is bound to be much variation from the schema proposed as no two persons are exactly the same. In addition there are many elements of the unexpected in human life. Every human being contains an unlimited potential for love and goodness which may emerge in unexpected directions. God is an incomprehensible Mystery who takes delight in unexpected interventions of love in each of our lives. Because of the variety of life's experiences, the older we are, the less exact will be the suggested times for progress from one stage of growth to another.

Crises of Growth

A crisis in growth refers to those points of decision that come in every person's life where a choice has to be made. To continue undisturbed in the same direction which one has been following in the past is no longer possible. There will usually be four options present: (1) escape from the crisis by regressing to an earlier and safer point of refuge; (2) become a fence-sitter and try to remain on dead center without going in either direction; (3) make a faulty or wrong choice; (4) make the right choice of action which enables progression from a childish level of personality to a new and higher stage of maturity and personality development.

Everything that we do—every decision we make—is important and affects our future growth in love and perfection, but there are certain times and particular decisions of life that are especially critical in the effect they have on our whole future. These decisions and these times in our life might be called "crises of growth". If we know ahead of time that these forks in the road are to be expected, we will be better able to cope with the crisis and make the right decision. Our own particular stages of growth may not have anything in common with this suggestion of a change each seven years. Nevertheless, everyone must face approximately the same stages of growth suggested at one time or another in life and usually in the order suggested. The more we know about these points of decision and the more we can learn from the experiences of others who have gone through similar crises of growth, the better equipped we will be to handle these important choices when they occur in our lives.

The path to maturity is nearly always painful. Some sufferings can be avoided by proper education and good experiences of unselfish love; but even the wisest, best prepared, and most loved person can expect crises, catastrophes, fear, bewilderment, anxiety, and mistakes. Our willingness to sacrifice our selfishness is the price necessary for growth. If we limit ourselves to the easy and attainable, we will stop growing. The really serious problems of life are never fully solved—growth in maturity comes from working incessantly upon them.

Naturally there will be certain key moments upon which the success of our future life's growth depends. It is important that we be ready for these moments when we find ourselves most free and the true masters of our destiny. Very often the experience of the nearness of death, either in oneself or in a loved one, presents the crisis necessary to destroy effectively the slavish power of the ego and awaken within us the true center of our being—the "self" or the "person."

At times of crisis the greatest dangers are discouragement or fear concerning the future coupled with a neurotic clinging to the past. Such fear stifles creativity and freedom and makes us over-protective of ourselves and our loved ones. Education, psychology, and love can help us overcome these fears; but ultimately continued growth toward maturity and sanctity will depend on the degree of our faith and trust in God.

Period of Youth (0-28)

THE FIRST STAGE OF LIFE, the period from birth to six or seven, begins with the crisis of birth itself. Even though a baby is helpless to do anything but accept whatever comes, it is important for parents to realize the tremendous shock that must be endured by the newborn individual. If there is great love and acceptance by the mother and all who handle this infant, this first crisis of life will be successfully resolved without future damage.

From birth then, until the age of six or seven, self-consciousness gradually awakens, as do knowledge, responsibility and freedom. Numerous experiences of unselfish love from the parents and all others who come in contact with the child will help to give a sense of security to the child who lacks inner defenses and must be protected from traumatic experiences. Reverence and respect for the person of God, for God's laws and the things that belong to God can be taught at this early age. A child will also learn to respect and love self as well as others if the parents and others the child meets have the proper respect for themselves, their own value as persons, as well as the value of other persons and things. In addition, personal responsibility can be developed through teaching the child to care for and keep in order the property entrusted to him or her. A child must be given the self-confidence to believe that through efforts at self-discipline one can learn to control oneself and attain perfection. The child must be constantly taught that this self-confidence comes through the help of God and one's own persevering, patient efforts to control oneself. A child learns more by example than by words to attain this happy balance between trust in God and trust in self.

THE SECOND STAGE OF YOUTH is from six to twelve or fourteen. Usually marking the crisis that begins this period is the entrance to school. The child begins to learn social consciousness through control of selfish desires and through consideration of the rights, privileges, and needs of others. A deep sense of responsibility for one's own actions and decisions is taught through the proper use of rewards and punishments that flow naturally as a result of certain actions. The value of self-discipline, self-control, and self-denial must be learned by means of thousands of little experiences of daily life and explained by the expert guidance of parents and teachers. A great love and respect for one's own freedom and the freedom of others can be attained through an appreciation of the happy results that flow from freedom and from the dangers involved in the use of freedom. A feeling of inner security and respect for one's own worth will be directly proportionate to the depth and number of experiences of unselfish love a child receives from parents and others with whom one associates at this age. One's ability to go out safely in love toward others is directly dependent upon one's own security.

THE THIRD STAGE OF YOUTH is from the age of puberty to one's legal coming of age around the age of 18-21. Besides the obvious problems connected with puberty and adolescence, this is the first time in life that a person becomes truly free to make decisions about life in general. It is the time when one makes those very important decisions about one's general attitude toward life, self, others, and God. One of the most important decisions of this period is the willingness to sacrifice "play" and accept the seriousness of purpose necessary to become a mature adult. One of the greatest dangers is for the youth to cling to the illusions and dreams of childhood and refuse to face the difficult facts of the world and life as they actually exist.

Before teen-age one is governed mostly by impulse and has few real problems. If a teen-ager is filled with inner fears, insecurity, and lack of trust in God and in his own worth, there is a danger that he or she will continue to cling obsessively to the ways of childhood and refuse to face the challenge of adulthood. A strong faith and trust in God and experiences of unselfish love given and received, plus a willingness to work hard and sacrifice oneself for the good of others, are the best solutions for developing a strong sense of responsibility.

Growth in self-consciousness makes a teen-ager aware of his or her own power, freedom, and value as a person. If one's parents and elders are unwilling to allow this budding of adulthood to mature, the inevitable conflicts between teen-agers and parents or adults will result. On the other hand, lack of experience, especially of failure, often makes the teen-ager over-optimistic about chances for success and causes one to underestimate the difficulties and struggles needed to succeed. Parents who try to satisfy every desire of their children are doing a terrible disservice to these children. Life thrives and matures when there is a good balance of pleasure and pain, hardship and ease, self-denial and self-indulgence, failure and success. Whereas life withers and growth in maturity is brought to a halt when there is too much of either pleasure or pain, failure or success, hardship or ease.

The teen-ager must learn to "feel" or experience both love from and toward others. If one has had good experiences of giving and receiving unselfish love during the previous years of childhood, one will find it less difficult to learn the complicated art of loving and being loved by others, especially those of the other sex. Even in the most favorable circumstance, the teen-ager needs to exercise much discipline, self-control, and self-denial in order to bring to maturity the awakening powers of love. Until now these powers have remained asleep within the depths of the inner being. Many difficulties can be expected as the budding adult struggles with his or her recently awakening sexuality. The awareness of the value of the person of the other sex becomes extremely fascinating and arouses curiosity. A tremendous attraction is felt for the need of the other sex to complement one's own one-sided personality. Physical attraction, sexual desires, a feeling of personal freedom and independence, and the newly awakened perception of the hidden values of persons and things—all contribute to the series of crises that mark this particular stage of growth.

THE FOURTH STAGE OF GROWTH FOR YOUTH occurs over a ten-year period between eighteen and twenty-eight. The real crisis experienced at this time is the event which cuts the umbilical cord that has previously tied one to one's home and family. This is the time when one makes a specific commitment and dedication of life to a particular cause, profession, or vocation. Similarly it is the usual time that one makes a commitment of self to a particular person in marriage. Youth ends and adulthood begins when one is ready and willing to take hold of one's future destiny, assume full responsibility for one's life, and make some kind of commitment of life's energies to some ideal or person.

This, then, is the time for one's conscious will to assume responsibility for one's future, take hold of one's existence, and make a solemn dedication of everything to a person or ideal other than oneself. This must be done regardless of the consequences. The more self-control and self-discipline one has developed in earlier life, the easier it will be to make this decision which plunges one into adult life. The more generous and unselfish is this decision, the easier and more certain it will be that the right decisions will be made in many other serious matters that will face one before death. Either directly or indirectly, one's commitment to unselfish love and service of others is actually a commitment to God as he is known at this time. Since God is love, a commitment to unselfish love and service to others is actually a commitment to God. Apart from God and love, life has no real meaning since it was for this we were created. The highest possible commitment is to carry on the work of love introduced into the world by the life, death, and resurrection of Jesus.

In general, the first period of life, from birth to age twenty-eight, is spent in the education of one's conscious faculties: senses, intellect, will, imagination, memory, feelings. Beginning with the knowledge of oneself as independent of others, around the age of two, the education and training of the conscious self (the ego) continues until a person is ready and willing to make a complete commitment of one's conscious faculties to some cause or person. To succeed in doing this one must develop a high degree of self-control and self-discipline. One's facility for getting along with others (i.e., training one's tools for community life) also needs to be developed. Other tasks of youth are learning responsibility; learning how to properly use one's freedom; developing one's abilities to think, reflect, and make good value judgments. One must also learn to handle feelings and emotions in a balanced way without losing control. Those young people who find it necessary to struggle hard to make ends meet materially and physically are usually spared deep inner problems, while those who are required to make few sacrifices and practice little self-discipline usually find it extremely difficult to assume the responsibilities of adult life. Instead they often remain in a state of permanent childishness or mediocrity throughout their adult years.

Period of Adulthood (28-56)

The middle period of life should be the time when one experiences the most growth. Unfortunately, many people imagine education ends with youth and adulthood is almost exclusively given to activity. If this idea is carried out in practice, not only does psychological and spiritual growth come to a halt, but a process of regression or return to childish immaturity also begins.

Whereas during the period of youth one has concentrated on the development of one's conscious faculties, the middle period of life from twenty-eight to fifty-six is the time to educate and develop one's unconscious faculties. If the tasks of youth have been successfully accomplished, one is ready, around the age of twenty-eight, to tackle the even more important tasks of adulthood by bringing to the level of consciousness the many undeveloped talents, resources, and energies that have until now remained asleep in the unconscious, inner being. The most important of these energies is the power to love. These reserves of love energy have four specific objectives: proper love for one's inner self; proper love and respect for God, the Supreme Being; proper love and respect for other individual human beings, especially those of the other sex; proper love and relationship with the community or communities of people to whom one belongs. These four tasks constitute the four stages of growth during the middle period of life. All four will require attention during these adult years, but ideally each of these tasks will constitute a stage of growth at this time of our life.

Authenticity (28-35)

Authenticity refers to the self-knowledge and acceptance of one's true nature and consists primarily of a proper balance and relationship between one's conscious and unconscious. We must strive to establish a correspondence between our external behavior and our true, inner being. Now is the proper time of life to delve beneath the surface of our consciousness and discover the blueprint of our life's destiny implanted by our Creator within the depths of our inner being. This means a voyage of self-discovery as well as a full acceptance of our real self with its challenges and its limitations. To become the person we have been destined to be will require a love and respect for our true self. It means leaving the charm and attractiveness of youth and entertaining the adult world of serious effort. Adult education means to "lead out" (e-ducare) the potential talents and energies stored in our unconscious inner being and to use whatever effort is required to put them to work in worthwhile causes. This means primarily a willingness to empty ourselves of mere self-serving and self-indulgence and to become servants of humanity. "Your attitude must be that of Christ; though he was by nature God, he emptied himself and took the form of a servant…He humbled himself becoming obedient unto death, even death on a cross" (Phil. 2:5-8).

At this stage of our growth into maturity we must above all else be willing to stand solidly in our truth and try not to escape into a dream world of non-reality. "To thine own self be true," says Shakespeare in "Hamlet." We must keep ourselves open to the intuitions and inspirations that arise from our inner being. This is the time to develop those sides of our personality that have previously remained uncultivated. We must learn the necessary skills for interpreting correctly the voice of our unconscious being and permit an easy flow of communication between the conscious and unconscious sides of our personality. Thus we become truly masters of our future being. As a result, we should experience a tremendous zest for life, an increase of both physical and psychic energy, new enthusiasm and creativity, along with a loss of fear and an increase of optimism for the future.

Adult Religious Conversion (30-40)

To attain a mature relationship with God we ordinarily experience some sort of crisis of faith. It is essential that as adults we experience a real freedom of choice between the options of belief and nonbelief. Serious doubts of faith concerning God and religion will challenge every mature adult. For a period of time one may experience real agnosticism or even a form of atheism. Having weighed all the options, a true religious conversion occurs when an adult freely chooses to make the leap of faith in a personal God. The Christian makes a further leap of faith to believe that God became man in the person of Jesus of Nazareth. The next step is the development of a deep, personal, intimate relationship of love, respect, a worship with God. Having accomplished the task of centering our life in the conscious will and in the inner self, we are now ready to center our life in God. When these three centering tasks are accomplished, we are ready to develop a basic philosophy of life to govern our conduct for the remaining years of our life. Such a religious philosophy will be based upon a free commitment of our life to God and to the service of God. Those who fail to make this complete gift of self to God choose instead some earthly ideal as their idol. If we do not choose God as the heart of everything in our life, we will choose some finite creature as our god. The alternative to God is either egotism whereby we make a god out of our conscious self, or materialism where we make a god of this world's goods, or secular humanism where we make a god of humanity.

The God of mature adulthood is quite different from the God we came to know in childhood. He is fascinating and awesome; gentle and demanding. It is not enough to have religious faith of children. As adults we should experience a personal encounter with the Supreme Being. But, before such an adult encounter is possible we must attain a mature knowledge of God as a real person capable of both giving and receiving a personal relationship of love. One of the tests that an adult encounter with God has been established is the growth of a mature and beautiful confidence in God and God's loving care.

Having come to know one's real, inner self with its vast potential which awaits development, we need confidence in the help of some higher power to enable us to attain the fulfillment of our capabilities. If there were only other human beings with similar weaknesses, there could be no real hope of success in our life. Only a faith and trust in a supreme being, higher and greater than ourselves, will give us the courage to struggle with our inner powers and attain maturity.

I-Thou Relationship (30-50)

The third stage of adult life is establishing a mature relationship with other individuals. One is capable of such a mature I-thou relationship only after successfully completing the previous tasks of self-control, the centering of one's life in one's inner self, and the commitment of this self to some higher cause. For this reason a really mature adult relationship of love usually develops only after the age of thirty. Sometimes, but not necessarily, such mature relationships occur with those with whom we have established youthful relationships. Thus serious problems of relationship frequently develop with married people between the ages of forty and fifty. Very lucky indeed are those couples who "find each other" after the children are grown or after economic problems are solved.

Having learned to confide in God, one is now ready to confide in another human being. There is always the risk of our love being rejected or abused when we make the gift of self to another person. Yet we must take this chance if we are to keep growing in maturity. Through the experience of human love given and received, many repressed areas of our unconscious will be discovered and developed. When these relationships are with persons of the other sex, the most observable development will be a good balance of masculinity and femininity.

If we choose not to make the sacrifice of one's self in love to another human being, our progress in maturity comes to a stop and we begin to regress into some form of childishness or spiritual sterility. Despite the risks of the I-thou relationships and commitments, no one can hope to reach full maturity on earth without the willingness and readiness to give oneself in love to others. If the person of forty or forty-five fails to confide himself or herself in love to another or other human beings, there is usually a serious regression into selfishness and mediocrity. One becomes prematurely old, barren and dry, hard and brittle, sour and bitter toward life. Some lose hope and withdraw into a shell and cut themselves off from their fellow human beings. Most of the vital energies of growth come to a halt. Idiosyncrasies that used to be funny now grow like cancer until they become a source of irritation to everyone. Greater and greater conservatism and fear of change are observable with a general negativism, pessimism, and resentment toward the whole world. Such a person often spends time criticizing and blaming others for all that is wrong in the world—blaming everyone but the real culprit, i.e., one's own refusal to give oneself in love to others.

On the other hand, the middle-aged person who is able to give himself or herself in unselfish love to others experiences a beautiful growth in character. One will discover many new powers never previously experienced: tenderness and sympathy for all those who suffer or who are in need; a willingness to change and adjust to others and to new situations. Being open to others through love opens one to other worthwhile values: God, truth, beauty, religion, the future. Instead of discouragement and pessimism, optimism and hope fill the one who loves. Enthusiasm, creativity, physical and psychic energy increase. By means of love one discovers the fountain of youth for which mankind has been searching from time immemorial.

I-We Relationship (40-56)

Having gained a certain ease or proficiency in individual I-thou relationships, a person is better able to establish good relationships with the various groups or communities to which one belongs. Learning good community relations begins when a child leaves home for school, and ability in community relations should develop throughout youth and adulthood. In middle age, a new need arises—i.e., to have groups to whom one can entrust the forward progress of the world after one's retirement from active life. We must assume the willingness to step back and confide and entrust others to carry on our pet projects. We must learn to work with a team. Instead of seeing others as rivals, we must learn to see them as partners. Through the community of our brethren we can accomplish much more than we could do alone. Realizing that alone we are unable to accomplish all the worthwhile objectives we have set for ourselves, we turn now with confidence to our brethren and entrust the future to them. Through our teaching and training of those younger than we, we confide and commit our dreams, hopes, and plans to the community. To do this we must see others as our equals, all dependent on one another. We adopt a sincere confidence in the youth of the next generation.

To attain good community relationships we need to have many adult experiences of our need of help from others and of their need of help from us. Only gradually as we have mature experience of our creatureliness and our dependence upon each other, do we experience the universal brotherhood of solidarity of the human race. We come to the realization that we are not self-sufficient, not capable of doing everything for ourselves. Advancing age and mature relationships of love can usually bring us to this point of putting our confidence in the group, in individuals whom we have learned to love, and above all in the power of God. Thus we are able to remain optimistic about the future even though we know that we personally will never be able to accomplish all the tasks that need to be done, or that we, when younger, had hoped to accomplish personally. The truly mature person is able to share with the community all that he has learned, all his hopes, all his dreams for the future. Similarly, he is not selfish about his accomplishments, realizing that they belong to the community and not just to himself. The hallmark of this period of life is the ability to confide, to commit and entrust oneself and the future to others, either as individuals or as a group.

Mature Adulthood (56 to death)

Unfortunately many people look upon this third period as the declining years. If the emphasis is placed upon activity and the production of visible, earthly results, this period of life will not be appreciated. Whereas, if one is willing to look at life on earth as a preparation for life in a higher, transcendent dimension of reality, then this final period becomes exceedingly important. Similarly, the higher we value the inner realities of life on earth—the things of the spirit—the more we will appreciate the importance of the period of retirement from active duty. If one has properly solved the previous tasks of maturity, there is no such thing as old age. Through spiritual maturity we become perpetually young, always growing, always open to the infinite riches of that transcendental dimension called God. Those who cooperate with God's graces and accept the unlimited challenges of their unconscious potential will find that life is not dull but becomes more interesting and joyful as we advance in years.

To prepare for old age we must become convinced that "being" is more important than "doing". This "being" should be primarily unselfish, completely forgetful of self, entirely other-centered, simple, humble and full of confidence. This is the way of spiritual childhood recommended by Jesus in the Gospel and practiced so beautifully by St. Therese of Lisieux. Such a love develops to the point of transparency whereby it radiates outward upon all who come in contact with it. Those filled with true love for God and neighbor become so transparent that their light shines on the whole of creation. Pope John XXIII was just such a person. Interestingly enough, it was only in his old age that people finally recognized the greatness of this man. All of his life had been a preparation for those few final years of old age when the transparency of his love revolutionized and transformed the church and the world.

Growth in Contemplation (56-63)

If one is to spend a fruitful old age, it is essential in the closing years of active life to shift attention more and more from busy worldly activity to hours of developing one's prayer life and union with God. An increase of faith in divine providence is required to give one the assurance that the Lord will in some way take care of all one's unfulfilled tasks, ambitions, hopes, dreams, plans, and desires. Through personal encounters of love with God, one gains this inner peace and certainty.

This is also the period of life to continue the gathering of disciples and persons of the younger generation with whom one can share one's wisdom and experience and to whom one can entrust the carrying on of the work begun. This also is the proper time to prepare for retirement from one's previous life's works by undertaking the needed preparation for some new apostolate of serving others—one that is in keeping with one's advanced years and decreasing physical energy. All of this requires a bold facing and acceptance of advancing years, declining strength, and nearness of death.

Retirement (63-70)

The more religiously oriented our earlier life was, the less critical will be the moment of retirement. Advanced age has been given to us for the final accomplishment of our religious and psychological perfection. To finish these tasks we need leisure and God has providentially made this possible through early retirement. Rather than resenting this inactivity, we should look forward with keen anticipation to these years. Spiritually speaking, they can and should be the most active years of our whole life. Therefore as we lay down the tools of our work, we should have some new task in keeping with our declining years to keep us busy. In some way this should consist in sharing with others the wisdom and experience we have gained throughout our life. This is also the time to put together the final edition of our philosophy of life which we can hope to leave as our main heritage to the next generation. Finally, this period of retirement from active life should be a period of intense growth in the unitive and mystical ways of prayer. St. Teresa of Avila speaks of seven mansions of union with God through which a mature, holy person should pass during life on earth. The first three mansions usually occupy our attention during the first sixty years of life. This leaves the higher mansions of mystical union with God to be accomplished during the final years of life after retirement.

Age of Wisdom (70-77)

This is the age of wisdom, age of faith, age of peace and mystical union with God through prayer. We need pure, blind faith in God at this period of life—a faith and confidence that enables us to put our hand in the hand of God, close our eyes and allow God to lead us where he will. This is a time to practice total abandonment of our life to God. St. Teresa of Avila calls this mystical union with God "spiritual marriage", i.e., a union with God similar to the union of man and woman in earthly marriage. If this happens, this will be a time of intense growth in the fruits of the Holy Spirit mentioned by St. Paul: "Love, joy, peace, patience, kindness, goodness, faithfulness, gentleness, moderation, self-control." Part of the joy of this stage of growth will be joy in the accomplishments of others. One's sense of solidarity with the rest of humanity will be so great that one rejoices as much in the good fortune and success of others as if it were one's own. Also the transparency of one's love for God and neighbor will be so apparent that there is no longer any need "to do" but simply "to be". This is what the Scriptures mean by Wisdom, the highest of all gifts of the Holy Spirit.

45

Facing Death (70-??)

All of life should be a dress rehearsal for death. From youth onward we need to be keenly aware of how fragile life is and how quickly it can be lost without the slightest forewarning. Throughout life we need to reflect upon death and live sufficiently detached from the things of this world so that we are willing to depart without looking back. The older we get and the more we realize that most of our life is behind us, the more foolish we are to act as though we were going to live forever on earth. If we have lived with the thought of death often enough throughout the years, the experience of the diminishments and weaknesses and perhaps pains which warn us of approaching death will not disturb us. Instead we look forward with peace and joy to the final consummation of our union with God in the great Beyond. We blindly entrust our whole future into God's loving care. Like St. Therese of Lisieux we look to "spend our heaven doing good on earth."

Summation

Every step that has been given for the various stages of growth is important and even necessary for full maturity. These tasks are often accomplished at an earlier or later age than the one suggested. However, there is a definite order to the steps by which we progress in the perfecting of our personality. If we attempt to impose too early a task of a later time or age, the result is sometimes disastrous. On the other hand, if we fail to complete a task at its proper time our obligation to accomplish it at some later date in life is not removed. This, of course, involves double or triple duty whereby we are accountable for the task of our appropriate age plus all the neglected tasks of earlier life. This explains why so few individuals reach full maturity in the present life. However, we must always strive to reach the fullest possible actualization of our potential.

CHAPTER FIVE

THE PLACE OF JESUS CHRIST
IN HUMAN MATURITY

When we make a psychological study of the Gospels, we discover that Jesus knew and lived the insights concerning human maturity that philosophers, psychologists, and other thinkers today are discovering. A study of the life of Jesus Christ reveals to us a picture of a fully mature human being and the personality of the whole person. In fact, one begins to realize that it is impossible to conceive of true maturity and sanctity apart from the teaching of Jesus. This does not mean that all Christians are necessarily more mature than non-Christians; rather it means that the goal of wholeness which God has destined for us can be seen most clearly in and through the person and teachings of Jesus. By reflection on the life, words, and actions of Jesus we are able to learn much of what is expected of us and how we too can attain wholeness.

In the first chapter of Genesis we are told that "God created man in the image of himself, in the image of God he created him" (Gen. 1:27). If we are to fulfill this image of God, it behooves us to study the most perfect of the images and expressions of God: Jesus Christ. When we are born, this image of perfection exists within the depths of our being as an ideal, which, to bring into actuality as we progress in age and development, requires many free choices on our part and God's constant helping graces.

The love of God and mankind manifested in the life, sufferings, and death of Jesus must be demonstrated to a secular world through the example of countless individual Christians. Otherwise, the meaning of love will grow dimmer and dimmer, and each generation will become historically more removed from the saving event of Jesus' life. Our responsibility, therefore, is to become Christ-like in the fullest possible sense. No individual human being can imitate Jesus totally in all the facets of Christ's infinite, divine personality. But, with experience and a certain amount of intuitive ability, we can transpose Jesus' life, as described in the Gospels, into the contemporary situation.

We must seek to identify ourselves with those particular elements in Christ's personality which strike a responsive chord in us and thus are in accord with the unique destiny for which we were created. Each individual must discover the particular "musical score" he is required to play in the giant symphony of praise to God that is meant to go up constantly from the whole of creation.

In the life of Jesus, there is a balance between those elements of a mature person which, at first sight, seem to contradict each other. Jesus exemplifies the proper balance between introversion and extraversion, sensation and intuition, intellect and feeling, spontaneity and good organization, masculinity and femininity, freedom and obedience. He admirably resolves the polarities of temperament and transcends these apparent opposites of human behavior by a beautiful unity of personality.

Jesus is the paradigm of the whole person, the prototype for all human development. There is a beautiful unity of the human and divine in his words and actions. He shows extraordinary ego strength along with humble submission to the higher will of his Father. Not only is there unity, simplicity, and adaptability in his life; there is also wholeness, integrity, and a beautiful order. He is able to associate with ease with the rich as well as with the poor, the uneducated as well as with those of the highest culture of his day. Yet, at crucial moments he retires into the desert to discover his inner direction and communes with his Heavenly Father. In each situation, even the most difficult, we see Jesus Christ making a free, mature decision. It is evident that he had complete command of his personality at all times, even when he expressed a deliberate and fully justified anger toward the Pharisees. His body and soul were subject to his will, which was in turn totally obedient to the will of his Father. Regardless of the circumstances, Jesus had confidence in himself and his ability to handle each situation in a way that would be pleasing to God and in accord with truth, justice, and charity. We see this especially when he was dealing with his enemies. Two examples would be: his answer to the Pharisees regarding paying tax to Caesar (Matt. 22:15-22) and the story of the woman taken in adultery and the insistence that Jesus pass judgment on her (John 8:1-11).

The Gospel of St. John, especially from Chapters Five to Twelve, is a beautiful description of how this mature, honest, and selfless man handled himself in the presence of hostility and opposition. There is no inferiority complex, no self-apology, no insecurity despite the fact that at the end of his life he was forced to stand alone with hardly a single friend to support him. Even in the depths of his passion and crucifixion, we find Jesus Christ filled with optimism and enthusiasm for the future. "I tell you that in the future you will see the Son of Man sitting at the right hand of the power of God and coming on the clouds of heaven (Matt. 26:64). He went to his death at peace with himself and with the absolute conviction that his Heavenly Father would vindicate him. "Father, into your hands I commend my spirit" (Lk. 23:46).

When we read the Gospels carefully, we are struck by the complete sincerity, openness and genuineness of Jesus. He hides behind no masks or false fronts. There is never any attempt to deceive or pretend to be different from what he actually is. Jesus was never self-seeking but always open to the needs and personality of others and did not force his companions to adjust themselves to his needs or conveniences. Rather, Jesus was willing to wait until those around him were able to face the awesomeness of his divine mission. He gives the impression of an inner peace and security which result in a gracefulness and a smooth functioning of the powers of his whole being. He possesses an extraordinary tranquility which indicates that everything is in its right place and that he has found the right place for everything in his great heart. He has accepted who he is, what he is meant to be, and is content to go about the work assigned to him. His all-consuming desire was to fulfill the tasks to which he had been sent to accomplish: Namely, to reveal the real nature of God, to proclaim God's kingdom, and to offer himself as a victim of love.

Jesus revealed to the world a new kind of God: a God of love who asks us to return good for evil, love for hatred, forgiveness for persecution; a God of truth who confronts people with their sins of oppression and self-seeking; yet who is so full of love that he personally suffers persecution and death at the hands of evil forces in order to experience first-hand the same fate his creatures often must face. When confronted by worldly powers, the love manifested by Jesus appeared weak and seemed vanquished; but by Jesus' resurrection, the love of God conquered the powers of this world, including both sin and death. "For God's folly is wiser than men, and his weakness is more powerful than men (I Cor. 1:25).

In Jesus we see a balance between love of God and love of neighbor. The brotherhood of mankind and divine filiation are of equal importance in the Gospel teaching of Jesus. In Jesus we see a divine love that is free and cannot be manipulated by anything other than a corresponding love from us. The first generations of Christians gave a special name to this new form of love: "Agape" from the Greek verb *agapan* which means to welcome, to be "wide open" in love to another. Later the name was given to the "love feast" which the first Christians celebrated in connection with the Eucharist. Agape (or agapistic love) came to mean the spontaneous, self-giving love expressed freely without calculation of cost or gain to the giver or merit in the receiver. It is the highest manifestation of Christian brotherly love as distinguished from erotic love which calculates its relation to others from the standpoint of its own need of others. At the Last Supper Jesus commanded his disciples to practice agape toward others: "A new commandment I give you, that you should love one another as I have loved you. By this shall all men know that you are my disciples" (John 13:34-35).

During his public ministry, Jesus used the concept of the Kingdom of God to explain God's love for us. For Jesus the Kingdom of God signified God's gracious act of forgiveness of the past, giving us a whole new beginning, wiping away our sins, accepting us as his beloved sons and daughters. The gift of the Kingdom makes us children of God sharing the same life of God that Jesus did. Since all other human beings share the same divine life, they automatically become our brothers and sisters. Jesus' Sermon on the Mount describes in detail what agape entails when directed toward other human beings.

The most distinctive trait of love exhibited by Jesus was for the poor, the suffering, the oppressed, the outcast, the forgotten, the little people of this world. There is no trace of racism or excessive nationalism in Jesus' love as we discover in reading the parable of the Good Samaritan and as displayed in his concern for the Samaritan woman at Jacob's well.

With the proclamation of the Kingdom, Jesus announced a whole new epoch of human history—a new way of God reaching to us and for us to reach out to other human beings. The "Good News" (Gospel) of God's gracious love places upon us the responsibility to show a graciousness and love to others. In the time of Jesus many people, especially the rich, the powerful, and the self-righteous, resisted the message of the Kingdom. They were envious of the poor, the sinners, the outcasts whom Jesus put on equal footing with the rich and powerful. Therefore, they opposed and contradicted his teachings concerning agapistic love. Gradually they won over to their side the majority of the people; half-way through his public ministry Jesus found himself abandoned except by a few faithful disciples. It would seem that even Jesus began to have doubts about the propriety of his message concerning the Kingdom. The eighth chapter of Mark's Gospel describes this Galilean crisis in the life of Jesus. Jesus left his ministry to his fellow Jews and went north into pagan territory with the Twelve. We can only speculate as to what temptations Jesus experienced. Perhaps at this time he came to realize fully that his God-given destiny was to suffer the fate of the Suffering Servant of Yahweh as described in the fifty-third chapter of Isaiah. In this struggle that faced Jesus we see clearly how a mature person should act in the face of frustration, opposition, and the failure of a project upon which he had set his heart. "He began to teach them that the Son of Man had to suffer much, be rejected by the elders, the chief priests, and the scribes, be put to death....He said these things quite openly" (Mark 8:31-32).

In the Paschal Mysteries of passion, death, and resurrection, Jesus fulfilled the third task of love which the Heavenly Father had sent him on earth to accomplish. "There is no greater love than this: to lay down one's life for one's friends" (John 15:13). As a victim of love, Jesus, by his death on the cross, brought to a focal point the whole Christ-event: the manifestation of God's absolutely unlimited love for his creatures and God's desire to unite all of us into that fullness of life and love which the Greeks call pleroma. On the cross Jesus' life seems to be a failure, and his teaching about the Kingdom of God a delusion. Even the Heavenly Father seems to have deserted him. "My God, my God, why have you abandoned me?" (Mark 15:34). However, his life had been lived with such unselfish devotion and integrity that he is finally won through to a resurrected body.

In Jesus the love of God for us has become historically tangible and thus irrevocable and absolutely explicit. Before the advent of Jesus Christ, this love was implicit in the world but somewhat uncertain. Through Jesus Christ we are able to encounter the person of God directly and through this contact with God receive power to overcome our weaknesses and limitations. We cannot hope to proclaim the love of God as clearly as Jesus, but our contribution to the redemption of our sinful world can nevertheless be real. Our love, insofar as it is Christ-like will be a redeeming love if it is a world-embracing and a world-uniting love opening to the transcendent life of God.

Sacred Scripture speaks of Jesus Christ as the "Word" or "Incarnation of God", which means that he perfectly expressed God's nature. However, the short lifetime of Jesus upon earth was not sufficient to express adequately the total fullness of God's infinite nature. Therefore all of us are called to be "incarnations" and "words" of God and to be Christ-like to the best of our ability thus bringing to a fuller expression the infinite, inexhaustible treasures of God. "So that the saints together make a unity…building up the body of Christ until the time comes when in the unity of a common faith and common knowledge of the Son of God, we arrive at real maturity—that measure of development which is meant by the fullness of Christ" (Eph. 4:12-14).

Because Jesus is the tangible, audible, visible expression of God in human flesh, he is the way by which we on earth can encounter God. Every association with the life of Jesus brings the grace to enable us to overcome our human weaknesses and rise to the high level of life required for maturity. Every word and action of Jesus is a sacrament which has the power to put us in direct contact with God and thus bring divine grace to our struggle against the obstacles along the path of life. Because of the blindness and disorder caused by sin, we cannot hope to reach full maturity without frequent contacts with Jesus Christ. Each time we expose ourselves in a receptive way to Jesus' words and actions in the Gospels, we absorb some of the divine energy that Jesus brought into the world. "It is him that God gives a full and complete expression of himself...moreover, *your own completeness is only realized in him*...God has made you to share in the very life of Christ...and *this is the only way in which we can reach our full growth in God*" (Col. 2:9,13,19).

Our personal relationship with Christ is capable of raising the psychic temperature of love in our inner world and in the outer world around us. If we are willing to open our being to the truth, goodness, and beauty of Jesus Christ, he will become a direct line of communication between God and ourselves. Through our emulation of Jesus we can become mature sons and daughters of our Heavenly Father. "We are not meant to remain as children at the mercy of every chance wind of doctrine or all the tricks men play in their cleverness in practicing deceit. If we live by the truth and in love, we shall grow in all ways into Christ who is the Head. For it is from the Head that the whole body, as a harmonious structure, is knit together by the joints with which it is provided, and grows by the proper functioning of its individual parts to its full maturity of love" (Eph. 4:14-16).

CHAPTER SIX

THE ART OF SELF-DISCIPLINE:
A BALANCED TENSION

St. Thomas Aquinas says that virtue stands in the middle between two opposing extremes. A balance between opposite poles runs as a constant theme throughout Christianity. This balance is the opposite of extremism or fanaticism which takes only one aspect of truth and exaggerates it while ignoring other opposing aspects. Heresy results from taking a particular insight while denying another equally true aspect of religion.

Christianity is based upon a conjunction of opposites: the divine versus the human nature of Jesus Christ; the cross versus the crown; earthly life versus heavenly life. The more we seek the holiness that makes us Christ-like, the harder we must strive to bring all our energies or powers into equilibrium. In fact, all of our life we should be working to bring into a balance all those opposites within our nature. Examples of such counterparts are: self-development/renunciation; self-expression/self-denial; happiness/suffering; attachment/detachment; body/spirit; activity/passivity; intellect/feeling; introversion/extraversion; positive/negative; male/female; life/death. Chapter Three of the Book of Ecclesiastes states this need for balance very poetically: "There is an appointed time for everything: a time for every affair under heaven...A time to seek and a time to lose; a time to keep and a time to cast away...."

Balance Between Self-Development and Renunciation

Development and renunciation—self-expression and self-denial—are not mutually exclusive but part of the general rhythm of growth from a lower to a higher level of maturity. They are like the breathing-in and breathing-out of our body: two components of a healthy, developing life but subject to an infinite number of subtle variations. The exact blending calls for spiritual tact and wisdom which need to be improved constantly. It is quite difficult to strike a proper harmony. We need a very high tension capacity to live under strain. Since self-discipline will increase our tension capacity, we need especially to emphasize self-denial. The fullest development of our potential occurs only when we willingly undergo pain and suffering, either by way of self-discipline or through the external circumstances in which we live. Those who lead an easy and comfortable existence often lack the will power and strength to live under heavy strain.

The best way to find where we need to diminish our egoistic self is to discover the things to which we are excessively attached, things about which we would be upset if they were suddenly removed from our lives. Examples of such excessive attachments are: alcohol, tobacco, coffee, drugs, sex, soft drinks, clothes, TV, golf, tennis, football, etc. We need to study our habits and discover the things upon which we spend time, money, and energy. How concerned would we be if one or other of these enjoyments were denied us? A good way to find the answer is to deny ourselves the enjoyment of one of these things for a period of time, for example, during the six weeks of Lent, and see how we react.

We should accept with gratitude and delight whatever pleasures and joys God's providence gives us; but let us not linger too long in the enjoyment of them. These physical indulgences leave the body physically worn out without the emotional surge of energy that nourishing restraint can provide. We need quite often to sacrifice bodily and worldly gratification to make room for the life of love to grow within us. We must strive to bring our whole self, both inner and outer, into subjection to the higher law of the universe, which is another way of saying "god's will". To do this we must keep a tension in our daily living between pleasure and pain, between struggle and rest, between attachment and detachment. Only by frequent constraint are we able to keep our human nature on an even keel and open to the diverse experiences needed for continued growth in wholeness.

The striving for higher values is not a case of masochistically diminishing our present enjoyment of earthly life. There is a definite place and a need for such pleasures. As the Book of Ecclesiastes says: "There is an appointed time for everything; a time to weep and a time to laugh; a time to mourn and a time to dance." We are not meant to be cold-blooded and unfeeling toward others but to feel a real attachment to loved ones; spouse, children, friends, relatives, country, etc. The personality becomes warped when one's whole life is filled with suffering and tragedy, just as all pleasure and no pain creates an imbalance in the opposite direction. We need discernment and wisdom to know when it is the right time for both. Self-denial does not mean repressing and destroying any of inner powers but simply controlling them and directing them into proper channels.

Christian asceticism does not thwart our highest, deepest, and greatest aspirations. To the contrary, our lesser and more ephemeral desires are sacrificed to make room for the higher and eternal aspirations. The road of life climbs upward and has a goal which is more spiritual than physical. Therefore, the highest possible spiritualizations which is the ultimate goal of life is not found in the temporal, material zones of this world but in a total transformation of ourselves into a wholeness similar to that of the risen Christ.

We need to go beyond the frontiers of the visible world and frequently sacrifice the good we now possess for the sake of the total "beyond." We need to transcend our earthly selves in order to reach the highest dimension of reality we call God.

There is more than a religious value to self-denial. Our psychological health demands it. People who live only for the satisfaction of their own selfish desires are disowned not only by the rest of mankind but are also rejected by their own inner self. They find themselves plagued by frustration, irritability, guilt, tension, fear, ugly moods, and unhappiness. The sooner we learn the difficult art of self-discipline, and the higher we develop our ability to endure pain and tension, the more quickly we will progress to maturity. Those who choose self-indulgence and the most comfortable life to bring their growth in wholeness to a halt and gradually regress into a more infantile way of life.

However, in our renunciation we must take care not to destroy or break our ego completely. It is vital that we maintain a certain tension and balance between a strong ego and a strong self-discipline. Both are important and both are needed for growth in wholeness and maturity. A total loss of ego-strength would allow the powerful forces of our unconscious to flood our conscious life and would bring about a breakdown of our psyche and result in a real psychosis. We need not be discouraged when we sometimes go to extremes in the matter of self-indulgence, for it seems that some strong personalities must suffer the humiliation of many falls in order to awaken them to reality and train them in proper balance. No one should ever presume to commit deliberate sin; but if sin should occur, even serious sin, there need be no discouragement. We must be willing to repent and try, try again.

There is a general tendency on the part of human nature to sloth and procrastination, especially when struggle and pain might be our lot. We must exercise our faculties of growth by limiting destructive egotistic desires every day.

58

Thousands of such decisions are required in a life-time. We need to break the chains of laziness, selfishness, greed, lust, gluttony. Basically these chains, which the New Testament often symbolizes by the word "world," promote the love of self to the exclusion of the love of God and neighbor.

The earlier in life we come to an understanding of the value of detachment and self-denial, the more quickly we will progress toward maturity and wholeness. Ideally, we learn self-discipline during the first twenty-five years of life, when we can best and most easily train our conscious faculties of mind, will, memory, feeling, and imagination. However, if for some reason, either through ignorance or neglect, we failed to master self-control of our conscious faculties during youth, we will need to accomplish this all-important task later in life. But the later we delay the practice of detachment, the more rigorous and lengthy the regime of self-discipline we will need. After the age of thirty we find ourselves burdened with other tasks of maturity and frequently those who have had a too comfortable and easy life in youth find themselves burdened with mental, emotional, psychological maladjustments during the middle years of their life. However, it is never too late to begin a program of self-discipline to bring about the needed integration of our inner faculties and attain a balance in our nature.

Freedom vs. Submission

One of the most basic reasons for practicing self-discipline is to experience the fullness of the freedom we need in order to love. Those persons who are not self-disciplined become slaves to whatever bodily or worldly desire they find themselves excessively attached. Only free persons are capable of love, since freedom allows one to make a free choice of giving oneself and one's life to this or that person or in this or that particular direction. To develop our potential for love we need to experience freedom and

59

detachment from the enemies of love: greed, egotism, and the excessive love of bodily pleasure. These are the three basic slaveries which prevent our attainment of maturity and sanctity and are the three basic temptations which Jesus suffered in the desert. All three center on the misuse of power. Only by humble submission and a transformation of these baser instincts do we obtain the freedom to love God, and our neighbor, and ourselves in the proper proportion.

The temptation of sensuality, avarice, and pride which Jesus encountered and mastered are the three basic desires all of us have to surmount. In all three instances we are dealing not with an absolute evil but rather a divinely created instinct which has a tendency to go to extremes and become a law unto itself. Instead of keeping to their proper functions as submissive servants to the total destiny of our life, they try to become independent of all control. Sensuality is when the instinct for self-preservation or the preservation of the species (sex) or the expression of honest love bow to a base, selfish expression. Greed is the instinct for freedom and independence expressed through the selfish hoarding of worldly possessions and power to the detriment of others. Pride is the instinct of self-love reigning supreme over duty to serve God and neighbor. In all these situations we are dealing with a great potential for good that resists submitting itself to higher aspiration.

In order to keep these instincts under control we must practice self-denial, detachment, and renunciation of excesses in each of these areas. Such renunciation may mean real pain and sacrifice of something we want very much; but this is the way to redeem these God-given instincts and free ourselves from slavery to self, to pleasure, to worldly goods. When we willingly accept the suffering involved in attaining freedom from these three forms of idolatry, we are "carrying our cross." Thus the cross becomes the symbol of the effort required for our growth from slavery to freedom.

Self-denial liberates the higher powers within us. The egocentric shell that we have built around our conscious life must be broken open in order to allow the bright sunlight of God's love to flood our whole being. Each time our egotism suffers a defeat we experience pain and frequently we imagine that we are losing something essential to our welfare. Actually, the opposite is true. Each time we give into our selfish desires for pleasure, material possessions, or worldly honors and ambitions, we become enslaved to these lesser powers and lose our freedom to practice the higher, spiritual powers. Either we allow ourselves to be possessed by love, or we will be possessed by things of this earth. This is another way of saying that we must sacrifice everything for Love, because God is Love (I John 4:8).

Fulfillment vs. Diminishment

A truly balanced life will have both fulfillment and diminishment. Unless we experience the fulfillment of at least some of our goals and objectives, we will become discouraged, bitter, and pessimistic. On the other hand, a person who never experiences failure will lose sight of his creatureliness and will rapidly assume the posture of a god. There is always a danger to those who are given power over the lives of their fellow human beings; and those who are invested with life-time positions of power are especially vulnerable to pride and arrogance. A mature balanced life will be a good mix of fulfillment and diminishment, of activity and passivity, of death and resurrection.

For many people there is no need to look for opportunities to practice diminishment. Divine providence provides them with ample opportunities through illness, pain, and physical, material, and spiritual losses. St. Paul states: "For those who love God, all things work together unto good" (Rom. 8:28). If we accept these uninvited crosses with patience and love, they will help us to establish the right priorities in our life and to reach the desired goal of wholeness. However, if they are accepted with resentment, they will hinder, not advance, our progress toward maturity. This does not mean that we are not allowed to use the ordinary common-sense means to eliminate these pains and losses from our life. Rather an attitude of detachment and a proper regard for the right priorities must be cultivated. We need to realize that there are other things that are more important than impoverishment and the avoidance of pain. The ability of loving acceptance is a more positive and productive power than freedom of pain.

One of the most valuable insights of our times is the increased appreciation of the dignity of man. At times, on the part of some, this appreciation has gone to the extreme of autonomy and independence of all restraint and submission. However, its finest expressions are seen in a better understanding of our responsibility to take control of our destiny and the destiny of the world and the struggle to keep us directed toward our goal of unity in love. This struggle requires laborious and persistent effort, and many times we are tempted to shirk our responsibilities. Irresponsibly we want to be relieved of the demands of our inner self, our neighbor, and God and wallow in selfish satisfaction and pursuits.

The inner direction of our heart is influenced by all the selfish decisions in our life. Past wrong decisions make us weak and vacillating in the present. A history of past selfishness requires many years of self-denial and acceptance of uninvited crosses of diminishment to change the direction of our heart from self toward God and love. Even after forgiveness, the evil effects of past excesses continue for a long time, even past our death into the lives of those who come after us. However, we must not be pessimistic about ourselves and our possibilities of success in our responsibilities of self-discipline. Instead, we must bravely face each new challenge, regardless of how often we may fail. There can be no permanent tragedy if, with humble confidence in the power of God, we keep trying.

CHAPTER SEVEN

OPENNESS TO CHANGE

No matter how mature we consider ourselves to be, we can never be satisfied with our past or present accomplishments. As long as we live, we should keep ourselves open to new personal growth, to new ideas, and to new crises or new points of decision. No matter how good a job we have done, we should be ready to leave what we have already accomplished and go on to something better. There is to be no excessive clinging to the past or even to the present.

It is impossible to know ahead of time all that God expects of us. We may have some general or even definite ideas of our mission on earth, but we should keep ourselves open to the ever-changing needs of the community and the historical situation of the world. We do not wait until we are absolutely certain of what we should do, because we cannot have absolute certitude about anything on earth. We will do whatever will do the most good for the most people, finding our satisfaction and joy in doing what we can to make others happy and bring them to the fulfillment of God's plan for the universe. We will make mistakes in our choice of what seems best; but as long as we keep ourselves open to any new manifestation of God's Spirit, we will surely fulfill our calling on earth.

Regardless of how long we may have followed a particular path or how difficult it might be to make a change in our way of life, we should be willing to leave our present place or attitude. Change must never be lightly made but only after we are reasonably convinced that we can do more good in some other endeavor. The point is that we are ready, like Abraham, to pick up and go elsewhere if it seems to be God's will.

This openness to new and perhaps better things requires us to rethink the assumptions upon which we have based our life. Instead of rigidly clinging to convictions and decisions made in the past, we should be willing to try new ways and new ideas. We are called to rethink our past presuppositions and determine if they apply in the same way to the problems of our present age and situation. Everything, both old and new, should be assessed, evaluated, and purified of superfluity and inefficiency. However, nothing old should be rejected without careful and prudent decision. The new is not always better and the old, worse. Openness always involves the risk of failure and the danger of making mistakes; but somehow we must find the courage to leave the comfortable harbor where our boat rests and launch forth into new, strange waters, and there let down our net for a fresh catch. "Launch out into the deep and let down your nets for a catch…and when they had done this, they caught an enormous shoal of fish, so big that the nets began to tear. So they signaled their friends in the other boat to come and help them. They came and filled the boats to the sinking point" (Lk. 5:4-7).

In this day of specialization, we are often forced to concentrate in a particular field. In addition to the variations of interest in our life's work, we should make ourselves aware of other things that are taking place in our community, our country, our church. We should choose a new area—whether it be politics, theology, psychology, or one of the arts—to explore and work at it until we have mastered it or at least garnered the information needed to satisfy our curiosity and needs. Then, we should pass on to another area of study and experience its dimensions. Again and again, in the course of a person's life, there should be a change in interests, in pursuit of knowledge, in goals and ambitions, in attitude and temperament. Otherwise, one's life becomes dull and uninteresting and we become stunted in our growth.

If we have been open to new pursuits, we will discover as we move through life that our temperament or personality has changed. This does not mean that our past way of acting was wrong. We have simply moved on to develop another area of potentiality. Those who fail to experience changes in attitudes and pursuits which result in changes in personality will find that their progress in maturity has come to a halt. In order to tap the variety of gifts we possess, we should concentrate for a time on one area of knowledge which will then cause some new growth in our personality and then shift our attention to some other area which will permit further growth.

In the course of our life we should experience many changes. The introduction of a new attitude or temperament does not mean that we have lost something. Rather, if we have the courage to hold on and keep progressing, we will soon discover the development of a beautiful balance in our personality as a result of this merger of the old and new. The balanced person is capable of using all four methods of experiencing truth: i.e., intellect, feeling, senses, and intuition. In early life we may find ourselves more adept with our senses than with intellect and feeling, and totally ignorant of our intuitions. Later, however, intellect and its development take our attention; still later feelings become the predominant way to learn new truth; and last of all, intuitive ability is recognized for its worth. As we mature, we will instinctively and automatically turn to the type of perception that is best suited for the occasion. When walking in the woods, or enjoying art and music, our sensation abilities will be fully attuned to every impression on the eyes, ears, and other senses. When studying a problem or arriving at a practical decision, our intellectual faculties will be fully awake. To arrive at a personal encounter with God or with a fellow human being, our feelings will be activated to their fullest possible degree. When we are open to God's Holy Spirit and God's inspirations during prayer, our intuitive perceptions will be actively at work.

One should develop an openness to the intuitions rising from our unconscious inner being which furnish direction to our conscious life. These intuitions are usually quite fleeting, so they must be caught and recognized at the moment they come, otherwise, we will repress them without realizing it. If we have taught ourselves not to be afraid of new things, an attitude of openness will pervade every part of our being. Our eyes, our ears, our mind, and our heart will be open to all that is good, true, and beautiful in God's creation. Our intuitions will be "on target". To be truly effective, this openness should remain with us from youth through old age, right up to death itself.

In order to arrive at the openness of personality necessary for wholeness, our many opposing qualities or virtues should work at peak capacity. We cannot be open to change without being confident, tenacious, and bold. These three attributes have a tendency to be overpowering and therefore need to be balanced with humility, meekness, and prudence.

Balance Between Confidence and Humility

For certain people and in certain situations, confidence in God and self-confidence need most to be emphasized. At other times humility is the virtue most needed for inner peace and security. For everyone and at all times, a certain tension must be kept between these two opposing virtues in order to attain the openness needed for personal growth.

The rate of growth of our personality is directly proportionate to the degree of inner peace we possess. This inner security results from a realization and appreciation of our value as a person along with a firm confidence in the loving care of God. If we are convinced of our own worth, we can trust our inner powers and grapple with the external realities of life. We will have confidence in ourselves and be willing to risk being open to change. We will be able to stand alone, if necessary, when everyone around us disagrees with us and opposes us.

Our self-confidence is usually the result of good experiences of love especially those received during childhood. If our parents, elders, and others truly believed in our worth; and if other people put their trust in us when we were younger; and finally, if we recollect the instances of God's loving care in the various crises of our life, we will have a self-confidence and inner security that enables us to meet with alacrity each new challenge of life. On the other hand, those who have been deprived of love and loving kindness in childhood and youth must accept, on faith, the wisdom, goodness, and love of God until they can interiorly experience God's loving care. Since God loves all of us unconditionally, one need not be afraid of being condemned for boldness or mistakes. As long as one is sincere in the desire to do what is right, one can trust God to protect us from any lasting harm. Trust in God results in a healthy self-confidence.

Every experience of unselfish love from another person will add to our self-confidence. The love of another, who sees us as we really are but still values us, will, more than anything else, build up our self-confidence. Conversely, when we reach out to others in unselfish love, we overcome our preoccupation with self, shake off our diffidence, and become more self-confident. Here we should take the risk of being open to people. So many wait for the other to make the first overture. If we lose our timidity just once and assert the self-confidence to initiate a friendship, we may be pleasantly surprised.

A lack of love from others does not make maturity impossible but simply adds to the challenge facing us and requires us to make an even greater effort. The very struggle to overcome insecurity can be the exact thing needed to reach our particular destiny in life. God is a master at taking the failures, struggles, wounds, and problems of life and arranging everything so that ultimately it redounds to our welfare.

If we have been denied experiences of unselfish love in the past, it is all the more necessary to make ourselves as lovable and attractive as possible through the perfection of those inner qualities of soul and personality that will draw others to us. There are many people who are willing to love us if we try to the best of our ability to become the lovable person God wants us to be. Rather than bemoan our failures or the mistakes of our parents and teachers, we should work to remedy whatever is now lacking in our character. We must believe that the loving providence of God can, and will, allow us to mend our mistakes and the failures of others who have hurt us.

If we go to others in humble service, we will discover that our inferiority complex is diminishing. If our life is occupied with unselfish love, we will experience a tremendous fulfillment. In the opportunities we have to give ourselves in loving service to others, God has provided a wonderful means to grow in inner peace and security. Regardless of what others may say, think, or do, if we keep trying to love and serve them as purely and sincerely as we can, we will soon realize that we are truly of value. We rise above a slavish dependence upon the good opinion of others and develop the peace and security needed for wholeness. No task will be too small or too humble for us to do for others. Jesus Christ, washing the feet of the disciples at the Last Supper, is our model: "If I, your teacher and Lord, have washed your feet, you ought to wash one another's feet. I have given you this example so that you may do as I have done" (John 13:14-15).

If our inner security is to continue throughout the adversities of life, it must be based on a strong confidence in God and a sincere and deep humility. Humility is the simple recognition and acceptance of our need for God's help and the help of others. We realize that what it means to be a creature—one who is filled with weaknesses and limitations and prone to failure and mistakes. This is the way we are made, and there is no need to feel devastated and discouraged because of our creatureliness. God asks only that we keep on trying to do what seems to be right; he will supply for our deficiencies. Knowing that it is human to fail, we will not be afraid to keep trying even in the face of repeated defeats. The best example of the triumph of failure is the death of Jesus Christ; that which seemed this greatest downfall was actually the means he used to redeem mankind!

If we are humble enough to admit our weaknesses and limitations and, at the same time, trust ourselves to God's loving care, we will find inner peace and confidence. The inwardly humble and God-trusting person is never afraid to be open to the changes necessary for maturation of personality.

Balance Between Tenacity and Meekness

No one attains maturity without heroic persistence in the struggles to attain that hoped-for goal. "He that perseveres to the end shall be saved" (Matt. 24:13). There is no place along the road to maturity for those who are easily discouraged. Because the price for growth is a life-long battle, we must gird ourselves with both tenacity and meekness to win the never-ending contest with ourselves, the world, and everything else that hinders us. The openness to change, essential to all growth, will show itself especially in the persistence and patience we show in the face of failure. Realizing that maturity comes at the end of a long struggle, we must be unyielding in our determination to keep trying for holiness as long as we live. This perseverance will show itself as a real stubbornness in our refusal to abandon the pursuit of those qualities needed for authenticity and wholeness.

There can be no true perseverance without a healthy attitude toward the work required. Those who are afraid of work or who are easily discouraged in the face of difficulty will never reach maturity. We must toil at the tasks of authenticity and maturity constantly, night and day, year after year, until the moment of death itself. The possibility of defeat will not deter us from tackling any task that seems worthwhile and important. As long as our conscience tells us that it is right, we keep trying even when those nearest and dearest to us disagree. At times we will stand alone without any human support except the testimony of our own convictions and conscience. What others may call plain stubbornness or bullheadedness can be the humble tenacity of a meek but courageous man or woman.

In no way should meekness ever imply weakness. Rather meekness is a sensitivity to everything of God—his love; his plans for us, for others, for the whole of his creation; the inspirations of his Holy Spirit. The meek person is ready to respond instantly to the least indication of God's will. Therefore, meekness is openness to change. This is the submissiveness of Christ: "I do always the things that please my Heavenly Father" (John 8:29). To attain meekness our minds and hearts should be completely open to both natural and supernatural truth. Through the practice of the love of God and others, we make our hearts tender and susceptible to the least movement of God's Spirit. Instead of being enslaved to ourselves or the things of the earth, the meek person has only one master: Jesus Christ, God Incarnate. The meek but tenacious person, who is independent of the world's glamour and pull, is the only one capable of being the true master and possessor of the earth (Cf. Matt. 5:5).

Balance Between Boldness and Prudence

Openness demands a boldness that is not afraid to be daring, to take chances, and to try new things. Yet our boldness should be balanced which uses reasonableness and intelligence to discover the best path to follow. Prudence dictates that we learn from our past experiences and seek the advice of friends and counselors who may be more objective and perceptive than we. A fearlessness based on common sense will know when to admit one is wrong and when to hold on to one's opinion, or when to seek another way and when to persevere stubbornly along the old and tried ways.

To keep a balance between boldness and prudence, between the need to launch forth into new waters and the need to wait for a more favorable opportunity, is not easy. The virtue of prudence requires not only the exercise of the wisdom of experience but also the use of our intuitive abilities to determine the right moment for acting and the right moment for waiting. The "eager beaver" who is always busy about some new project is usually one possessed with an "energy neurosis" or is a "workaholic". As one becomes more mature, the more one will realize that periods of repose are needed for new ideas to germinate and for new energy to be generated within us.

Somehow, either from within or without, we will find the help to face each new problem or situation of life as it arises and find a proper solution to it. With faith and hope in God, we can believe that no situation in life is impossible of solution. The answer frequently will be different from the one we might have expected, but there is always a way out of every problem. "God is faithful, he will never allow you to be tempted more than you are able to bear, but with every temptation he will take issue with it and give you a way out" (I Cor. 10:13).

To grow in openness we should be willing to take chances and run the risk of failure with its usual feelings of

71

guilt. This is the risk we take to grow to be mature sons and daughters of God. Those who are filled with fear and refuse to risk themselves in the pursuit of wholeness will never attain the goal. "I am ready for anything through the strength of the one who lives within me" (Phil. 4:13).

A good example of openness for us to reflect on is Abraham, the Father of Our Faith. God did not tell him where he was to go but only to leave his present home and "go to the place I will show you" (Gen. 12:1). Because Abraham was completely open and humble, there was no hesitation but total acceptance of what God asked. Even when told to take his only son and present him as a burnt offering (Gen. 22:2), Abraham obeyed at once. Such meekness and tenacious commitment should give us the boldness and self-confidence to "slay our darlings" and, if necessary, to leave the place, the things, and even the persons we love and go to whatever new place God calls us. This new place is not necessarily a part of the external world but very often may be in the inner depths of our being. The life of each one of us is lived both outwardly and inwardly, that is, both consciously and unconsciously. We should be aware of these two "places" of existence and be willing and courageous enough to develop each one and bring all its possibilities and potentialities in balance with the other.

CHAPTER EIGHT

BALANCE BETWEEN OUR EGO AND THE SELF

To establish a proper balance between our conscious and unconscious, we must find the right relationship between the "I" of our conscious life and the inner center of our being which is called the "self" by Jung and the "person" by existential philosophers. In a mature person, the faculties of conscious life are centered in one focal point which we call the "ego." At the same time, the powers of the unconscious find a center in the inner self which we will call the "person." A balance must be found between the ego and the person with the ego subject to the person as a lesser prince or executive officer might be to a king. Because the unconscious powers within us are so powerful, it is the inner self or person which ultimately determines the direction our life will take. However, since this inner self is buried below the level of consciousness and awakens somewhat later in life than does the ego, one of the greatest problems seems to be the establishment and maintenance of the proper order between the ego of consciousness and the inner self or person.

The ego awakens rather early in life, usually around the age of two, when a child first uses the word "I" to refer to itself. Throughout the first 25 years of life our primary task is the education of the conscious part of life. Anything of which we are consciously aware should be centered at one focal point—the "I" or ego. This process of centering is called self-discipline, self-control. Because the ego has such a vital part to play in the development of the mind, will, and other conscious faculties, there is a danger that the ego will become the sole ruler of our life. It is in accord with the right order of maturation when the ego controls our motivations and decisions until sometime after the age of puberty.

Beginning in the teen years, frequently at the time of one's first experience of love with the other sex, the normal human being experiences emotions over which he or she has little control. Certain feelings of which one had never previously been aware rise to the surface of consciousness. About the same time, one's ego finds that it is no longer able to exercise the complete control over life that perhaps it had been able to do previously. As St. Paul puts it, "I often find that I have the will to do good but not the power. The good I want to do, I don't accomplish and the evil I don't really want to do, I find myself doing" (Rom. 7:15-16). What St. Paul so vividly describes is an experience that comes to every human being many times in the course of life on earth. The ego is never able to maintain absolute mastery over our life.

What is happening at these times? The inner world called the unconscious is beginning to awaken. At first, these stirrings of the unconscious are vague and disorganized. To mature we must organize these new powers around a focal point; but this cannot be the ego. The ego is simply incapable of handling and controlling these stronger and more complicated powers of our inner being. A new center to our life must be found—one that can control both our unconscious as well as our conscious life, one that resides in the depths of our being. A variety of names has been given to this center. Existentialists and other philosophers call it the "person." Depth psychologists call it the "self," meaning the inner self as distinguished from the ego which is the outer, conscious self. When we view the external manifestations of the inner person we call it the "personality." Sacred Scripture frequently speaks of the inner self as the "heart" of man. A number of the old spiritual writers used the term *scintilla* to describe the person. This is a Latin word meaning a spark of fire, darting forth from a much larger flame. In the minds of the spiritual writers, our inner person is the spark of divinity which God has implanted in our breasts to enable us to become truly God-like. We may think of it either as the highest peak of our being or the deepest well-spring of our soul. Jung frequently distinguishes between the personal self which is the center of each human being and the divine "Self" which is the image of God each of us carries within ourselves.

It is difficult to exaggerate the importance and value of each individual person. Every person was created by God to express a particular divine idea. Each human person is capable of sharing the divine life of love lived by the Father, Son and Holy Spirit. There is a uniqueness about every human person that makes each one of us absolutely irreplaceable. Each person is a reflection of God, yet always in a different way from every other person. For this reason the particular wholeness each of us attains will be somewhat different from that of all other human beings. To emphasize the uniqueness of each person C. G. Jung called the process of maturation "individuation." We can learn much from the experience of others about how to bring our person to maturity, but our personal responsibility is to discover the unique divine image or "idea" God has destined for us. This individuality of our person makes every personal relationship with others new and interesting. We are intrigued by the mysteries hidden behind each personality. No matter how well we think we know the other, we can always expect surprises, especially if the other one has developed his or her personality to a high degree of maturity. Once we have come to know the person of another, we know that it is impossible for anyone to replace him or her in our life. Intellect, strength, experience, education—all can be replaced; but there is no other person who can take our place, either in the presence of God or in the circle of friends who know us as a person rather than just a thing.

When we are born, our inner person is asleep. In childhood the center of our life is usually outside ourselves; first it is a parent, then a teacher or friend whom we admire, or perhaps a hero or heroine about whom we have read in books. During youth and adolescence there is a fusion of the many ideals of our life into a unity to which Freud gave the name, "super-ego." This combination of the conscience of our parents and the rules for right living absorbed from the culture around us is a truly valid factor in the development of our personality. However, it is not enough. To bring us to adulthood a new center for our life must be found within us rather than focused upon some outside person or ideal -- i.e., our motivation must be "our own." This inner core should integrate all those worthwhile ideals that have influenced us in our earlier life and unite them with the goals that now challenge us in adult life. In this process of integration we will often find it necessary to cast aside a former ideal that is false to our true inner nature; and if we have the courage and self-confidence to keep changing, we can hope to become the true master of our destiny and the keeper of our soul-castle. Once this inner self with its unconscious powers and tremendous potential is awakened, an even greater struggle is required to attain a balanced control over them. We must work hard to center our conscious and unconscious life around our inner person so that it may become the real king and center of our being. This process is a task that continues as long as we live.

Many people never get past the stage of centering their life in their conscious ego. They try to live their lives exclusively on the conscious level. However, after the age of 30 or 35, they find that the ego becomes less and less capable of doing a good job of self-control. Even when the ego succeeds in accomplishing the necessary centering and disciplining of the conscious faculties, there is still the danger that the ego will attempt to become the king and center of our whole life. When this happens, we are faced with the most common of all faults of mankind: "egotism," or, as it is more commonly called, selfishness or pride.

If we fail to look beyond the ego for the center of our life, we can expect one of several results: a constantly mounting internal chaos and disorder; a repression of the inner life-forces of spiritual and psychological growth; serious emotional disturbances; or a complete breakdown of mental health. In order to arrive at full maturity, a way must be found to break through the hard shell of egocentricity that has a tendency to grow around our conscious life.

Only the inner self is the trustworthy controller of our whole nature. This highest peak of our being has a voice that can speak; we call it "our conscience." It is not always possible to distinguish the voice of the conscience from the selfish voice of the ego. However, the more mature and integrated our personality becomes, the more easily we can recognize this voice of the inner self and obey it. Like the rest of our nature, our conscience also needs to be trained and educated. In our day, when there is so much emphasis on freedom and responsibility of the individual, the right formation of conscience is one of the most important tasks facing mankind.

If the work of maturation is to proceed with due speed, it is essential to establish a good and harmonious partnership between the conscious ego and the inner person. The ego must be trained to act as an explorer who makes frequent journeys into the hidden recesses of our unconscious being and brings into conscious life all that it finds there. Each new discovery will result in a certain crisis of adjustment with the counterpart in our conscious life. By self-discipline, struggle, and hard work we can train the ego to be a dutiful servant who obeys the voice of the inner self rather than pleases only our conscious selfish desires.

In the mature person, the conscious ego will be the external reflection of the inner person and will carry out its wishes. In the immature person, the ego yields to selfishness and rejects the more altruistic depths of one's inner likeness to God. Each year of our life should find our inner self more awakened and actualized at a higher level of maturity. If the inner self is not our true master and leader, our life and relationship with God and others will be superficial, impersonal, easily broken or changed. Our only interest will be to please our conscious ego. We may carry out reasonably well the external obligations we have toward God and our fellow-men; but they will not be motivated by any real love. Our service will be bound by an egotistic hope of reward or fear of losing someone or something we need for our earthly welfare rather than by the true freedom of mature love.

Freedom exists primarily in the inner person; and only when our faculties are under the control of the deeper self are we truly self-possessed and free. This freedom is manifested when we are able to take hold of our whole life and existence and make a gift of them to another person or persons in a personal encounter of love. The more centered our life is in the inner person, the more capable are we of giving and receiving this total gift of love.

One of the greatest weaknesses of the egocentric person is the inability to live on a personal level with another person. The egotist has the tendency to treat others as things to be used for personal aggrandizement. Without respecting the dignity and freedom of others, such a person attempts to force his or her selfish desires upon them in the same way as one would use a physical tool to accomplish some needed task. Anything not subject to the conscious ego is ignored. As a result, most of the vital functions of the soul are inhibited. Unable to handle effectively these unconscious powers, the ego feels an insecurity and inadequacy. Such an unprotected ego is constantly endangered from within by its own unconscious fears and from without by other egocentric people.

The selfish, ego-centered person is irritable, nervous, deeply insecure, and uncertain. He or she becomes excessively afraid of failure and overestimates the energy needed to succeed. Each new task imposes an added strain upon the already overworked egocentric tensions. Energy that could be used in a constructive way is drained off into vain struggles to protect a precarious egotistical freedom. Whatever creative ability one might have had disappears. The egotist is unwilling to run the risk of mistakes and failure necessary to guarantee success. Anything that endangers one's shaky position must be avoided. "I must not fail. I must succeed at any cost. I must win the praise and approval of all." This attitude results in an inability to make decisions, to show emotion, or even to experience deep feelings. Such a person cannot think clearly and acts as though he or she were carrying an invisible but heavy weight. His burden of egocentric fears and anxieties results in an unhappy, non-productive, impersonal existence.

How can we break the vicious circle of egotism that is often passed on from one selfish generation to another? How can we convince ourselves that the superficialities of an ego-centered life leave us bereft of a truly integrated and wholesome existence? How can we wrest control from the ego and become better balanced with our inner self? How can we uncover the person and make it the true center of our life? To bring about the necessary balance the first and most important step is a better knowledge and understanding of the inner workings of our personality. We need to know as much as possible about the true nature of the ego and the person and what their real functions should be in a mature personality. We call this self-knowledge or authenticity.

CHAPTER NINE

SELF-KNOWLEDGE OR AUTHENTICITY

The first step to authenticity and genuineness is to desire and accept the truth about ourselves and then to live in accord with this reality. Authenticity means knowing both the bad as well as the good about ourselves. To find the courage to face the evil within us, our growth in self-knowledge must be kept in balance with a realization of our good qualities and our vast potential for good. Otherwise, we will be filled with depression and discouragement at the thought of our failures and lack the courage to pursue the truth further. Those who fail to see the many things of value and worth in their nature will usually find that they are repressing certain facts about their shortcomings and hiding them from their own conscious view as well as that of others.

Our desire to be honest must be even greater than our desire to be good. In no way does this mean that we turn our back on God or goodness; rather it is the realization that the only way to any authentic virtue is by way of the truth. The task of discovering the truth about ourselves is never finished. Regardless of how honest we have tried to be in the past, we can presume we are still in some way, consciously or unconsciously, deceiving ourselves about our limitations, weaknesses, and faults. Our aim must be to eliminate this self-deception as far as possible. If we keep working at it, we will continue to progress on the road to authenticity; and this is enough to preserve our psychic health and to keep us growing in maturity.

To give us the incentive to pay the price necessary to obtain the truth about ourselves, we should meditate upon the words of Christ: "You shall know the truth and the truth shall make you free" (Jn. 8:32). As long as we are in the dark about our real nature, we will be enslaved to fear and at the mercy of our egotism or easily led astray by another egocentric person. We will be a spiritually and psychologically healthy person only when we live according to our inner truth. This means that authenticity is present to the extent that our conscious life is in accord with our unconscious and hidden self. To be false to this true center of our being is to live a lie; none of us will ever be happy and at peace as long as we live thusly. We may succeed in deceiving our conscious mind and may even be successful in deceiving our neighbors, but never can we deceive our inner person.

To reach wholeness it is necessary that our exterior conduct corresponds to the particular idea or image which God has implanted in the depths of our soul. We are authentic when we are the true expression of God's plan for us. To possess the fullness of truth would mean that we know fully our destiny in life and the tasks required to attain this goal. This is, of course, impossible this side of the grave. Authenticity will be present when we know where we now are on the road to wholeness and the next immediate steps we should take to progress toward our destined goal.

Each of us is called to carry out those tasks in life which will make the greatest possible contribution to the welfare of others and the increase of God's kingdom on earth. To fulfill this destiny, it is necessary to discover which particular expression of God's truth, beauty, goodness, and life we can best exemplify. We need to realize that we have not been created for ourselves but for God, for others, and for the world. We find our happiness and satisfaction only when we discover the contributions we are to make to the welfare of society and sincerely try to fulfill them. Regardless of how contrary to our own selfish desires this destiny might be, it is to our advantage and to the advantage of society if we try to discover what accomplishes our potential for good. We must use intelligence, prudence, courage, and intuitions, as well as the help of friends and counselors to discover what is indeed best for us.

When two, stringed musical instruments are perfectly attuned to each other, a note struck on one will cause the other immediately to vibrate the same sound. For example, if a piano and a violin are exactly in tune, any note struck on the piano will be heard on the violin without anyone touching the strings of the instrument. Our task in life is to keep ourselves so perfectly attuned to God's will that we begin at once to sound each new note which God strikes. God's call to us is like the notes of a special melody for an instrument of a symphony orchestra. If we play the particular musical notes revealed to us by our conscience and common sense, we will find ourselves a part of a universal symphony of praise, love, gratitude, and adoration continually going up to God from the whole of creation. What is more, this great symphony will also fulfill the deepest needs, desires, and goals of ourselves and our brethren.

Each of us has a special part to carry out in this great concert of praise and glory to God. Each has a unique instrument upon which to play the score assigned to us. Daily we are given a new melody to learn. We must not choose according to our own desires but rather accept the melody revealed by God's providence. If we try to play another's score or one different from God's will for us, our contribution to the symphony of creation will be a cacophony instead of a harmony, a sour or artificial note instead of a sweet true melody. Even though we imagine that the vocation of some other person is better than our own, we will hinder the total work of God upon earth if we deliberately try to play a different instrument or a different musical score from the one assigned to us.

It is not easy to discover the particular melody God wills for us; and once we know the melody, it is often difficult to play the score assigned to us. Authenticity is never perfectly attained on earth; we are always in the process of "becoming." We must keep changing, improving, refining, and perfecting our way of life. We can expect to make many mistakes, to play many false notes while practicing for our role in God's eternal symphony of praise. Our task on earth is to become the best possible instrument of God's will and to prepare ourselves as best we can to play our part in the great concert which the whole of renewed creation will present to God on the Last Day. To be ready for this final destiny we must keep practicing every day. If we realize that we are using the wrong score, we must make a change, no matter how late in life we discover the error. No matter how insignificant our part may seem to be, the important thing is that it be authentic and not an artificial one invented by us or borrowed from someone else.

If we succeed in standing solidly in our truth, no matter how insignificant it might seem, we will possess a charming naturalness and openness of character that will make us quite attractive and pleasing to others. There will be a simplicity and straight-forwardness about us that will make life much easier than when one is constantly seeking to live a lie or to live some way of life other than the one destined for us. No matter how strange, peculiar, or unique we might find our real destiny to be, we must strive to be true to it if we wish to be whole and happy.

If we are intelligent, we will realize that it is impossible to repress or destroy completely anything that is real within us. To repress something unpleasant is as senseless as pushing a splinter deeper into our finger so that we can't see it. This does not rid of us the problem but simply puts off the final solution. In the meantime there will be a substantial increase of pain and additional difficulty of solution. Most neuroses have their origin in a vain attempt to push our unsolved fears or faults into the unconscious and thus forget them. This is a dishonest way of refusing to face the truth, and nature will not allow us to live a life of falsehood indefinitely. The repressed truth festers below the level of consciousness and finally erupts in bad dreams, psychological blunders, uncontrolled fears, anxieties, and other mental illnesses or emotional disturbances.

To arrive at authenticity, we must openly work with our faults and problems until we find a way to change the direction of their energy so that some worthwhile goal can be found for them. However, we must be careful not to bring all the truth too quickly to the surface of consciousness. The poison of dishonesty and insincerity must be gradually exposed and expelled; otherwise our bodily, mental, and emotional health will be endangered by the traumatic experience of suddenly seeing ourselves as we really are. Those who are unwilling to face this exposure of the truth about their real nature will frequently have dreams of appearing naked on the street or before other people. This is a symbolic manifestation of their foolish fear of being uncovered and shown in public as worthless or unimportant.

We should have no illusions about the problems and even the dangers involved in tearing away the masks of falsity behind which our authentic self is hidden. When we reveal the unconscious depths of our true self, it will seem as though we were opening a Pandora's Box that threatens us with all kinds of disasters and ills. However, if we want to become whole, we must find the courage to open this box and face the consequences. We must not turn away in disgust from what is revealed but be willing to study these faults, discover their origins, and their peculiar characteristics. We must admit the tricks by which our ego deceives our intellect and leads us and others astray about our true nature. Knowing the unlimited capabilities for good or evil that exist in every human heart, we should not be surprised at any possibility of evil that might exist in us. Goethe writes: "With the slightest shift in the balance of our nature there is no crime of which we are not capable." We can find encouragement in the realization that human nature is fundamentally good. If we try to be truly genuine, all of the energy that we previously wasted trying to hide our faults can be utilized for good.

We often need the help of others to arrive at this knowledge of our own true nature. It is extremely difficult and often impossible to expose the unconscious depths of our soul without the help and guidance of some other person who acts as an interpreter or therapist for us. This person need not be a professional therapist; but, if possible, he or she should be someone who has substantially accomplished the work of authenticity in his or her own inner being. However, because friends and advisors are so essential for growth in authenticity, we should accept the aid of anyone who shows a sincere and unselfish desire and willingness to help us learn the truth about ourselves.

If we hope to get help from a counselor or friend, we must be absolutely open in admitting the bad as well as the good we see in ourselves. If we hold back something of which we are ashamed, we are wasting our time and the time of the therapist, spiritual director, counselor, or friend whose help we have sought. To be healed of the wounds of our past sins, we must be willing to confess our faults to some other human being. Open confession is necessary because we do not really recognize the full truth about ourselves until we have shared this knowledge with at least one other person who agrees with us that it is the truth. Once our friend or counselor has heard our tale of woe and agrees that we should be ashamed of it, it is never again possible to lose sight of this truth. Whereas, if we keep our secret to ourselves, even if we confess it in secret to God, the chances are that sooner or later we will tone down the admission of our guilt and find some way to justify our past sinful actions.

To confess our faults and weaknesses to just anyone would be harmful. We should seek out a trustworthy person who will not abuse our confidence or use the knowledge against us. Having heard our confession, the confessor gains a certain power over us. If he or she is a selfish or unscrupulous person, he or she may be tempted to use this power for egotistic satisfaction. The "friend" may enjoy exerting an undue influence over us to make up for his or her inability to control his or her own inner being and admit his or her own truth. Therefore, we should take special pains to make sure that our counselor is as genuinely unselfish and as authentic as possible—that is, one who is truly interested in our welfare and who is willing to guide us through the suffering, fear, anxiety, and anguish of our admitted guilt to a new level of wholeness and health.

Often the truth comes to us when we are off guard, at an unpropitious moment or from some unexpected source. Sometimes just listening to others criticize us will help us find the truth about ourselves. Instead of being angry or hurt when someone tells us our faults, we should try to accept as graciously as possible the things they say. Unless our desire and love for the truth is really intense, we will frequently reject this criticism and opportunity to change and grow. Once we rebuff another who tries to tell us of our faults, the chances are that this "friend" will not make a second attempt to help us. Therefore, instead of showing resentment or making excuses for our actions when we are criticized, we should sincerely urge others to tell us what is wrong with us. We need not accept at face value every possible objection that they express. Nevertheless, we should seriously consider their suggestions and try to discover what is true and what is exaggerated. With this attitude, we often discover that our supposed enemies are actually our benefactors in the sense that they tell us the truth we need to know about ourselves.

If our love for the truth is genuine, we will keep ourselves open to every opportunity to grow in knowledge of ourselves. We will pray frequently to God to show us the truth, to give us the courage to face it, and to do something constructive about it. Having prayed, we will keep ourselves open to whatever inspirations and intuitions that might come our way. Through the voice of conscience, the words of others, and the events of divine providence, God will speak to us and show us the way. It is not for us to choose the time and the place for learning the truth; we must be always ready and willing to be humbled by some new and unexpected revelation about ourselves. If we sincerely want the truth, we can be reasonably certain that God will provide it.

To help us persevere in our growth in authenticity, we need enough faith and trust in God to be convinced that nothing but good can come from the revelation of the truth. We should be encouraged by God's love for the sinner and his desire to forgive and show mercy. As believers, we know that God has called all of us, especially sinners, to repentance and forgiveness. Regardless of how dishonest or shameful we might have been in the past, God will still help us attain truth and perfection. We need only to admit our guilt, be sorry for it, and work diligently in the future to show our love for God and others. God will do the rest.

"O my God, relying on your almighty power and infinite goodness and promises, I hope to obtain pardon of my sins, the help of your grace and life everlasting, through the merits of Jesus Christ, my Lord and Redeemer." (Act of Hope)

To conceive of any kind of valid maturity without authenticity or self-knowledge is impossible. So intimately connected are truth and maturity that they might almost be considered synonyms for the same reality. Every step in authenticity will result automatically in a corresponding growth in the wholeness and integrity of our personality. If we squarely and sincerely face each unpleasant or humiliating truth about ourselves, we will discover that through a certain conversion of energy, we will be able to transform every failure into a means of new growth in virtue and perfection. Knowing the truth about ourselves is half the battle in overcoming our egotism and bringing about the required balance between our conscious and unconscious lives. The first step in discovering this truth is recognizing and resolving the unconscious masks we all wear.

CHAPTER TEN

YOUR MASK IS SHOWING!

Others can help us find our vocation in life, but ultimately we are responsible for making our own decisions. Of one thing we can be certain; God does not want us to echo the melody some other human being has lived, no matter how perfect or authentic it might seem to be. We can learn much from the examples of great saints and other mature people, but we must never pattern our life exactly on theirs. If we attempt to do so, we will find ourselves contributing to a cacophony instead of a symphony of praise to God; and our life will be untrue and lacking in authenticity. When we try to follow a life alien to our nature, we lose our naturalness and simplicity and find ourselves fettered and shackled by artificiality and unreality.

Jung has given the name of "mask" or "persona" to this unconscious artificiality possessed by so many people in our modern world. To wear a psychological mask is to attempt unconsciously to play a role in society other than the authentic task assigned to us by God. The mask is always unconscious. The moment we become fully aware that we are playing a role, it is no longer a mask, as the depth psychologists understand it. To wear a mask is quite different from knowingly and deliberately fulfilling a particular function that might be required of us in various situations. For example, anyone who is called upon to exercise authority must assume a role higher than his own intrinsic person. Parents must represent the authority of God to their young children; a judge or policeman represents the authority of the state; clergymen and teachers should speak for an authority greater than themselves. Sometimes to give other people strength we must play a character role stronger than we really are. Members of large corporations often need to play roles commensurate with their particular business position. Officers in the armed forces and other government officials are required to fulfill a position that is greater than their individual strength. As long as we are consciously and vividly aware that we are living a part different from our authentic self, this charade will do us no harm. It is often essential for the successful accomplishment of community living.

Whenever we forget that the part we are playing is not our real self and imagine this role is our true reality, the persona develops. It comes as a real shock to most of us when depth psychologists maintain that everyone wears unconscious masks and plays roles different from the authentic tasks assigned them by God's providence. To put this another way, there is a certain amount of artificiality in the lives of all of us. To be conscious of any real falsity in our lives is bad enough; but it is even more dangerous when this hypocrisy is present without our knowing it. As long as we realize that we lack authenticity, we can do something about it if we so choose. However, the person wearing an unconscious mask is totally helpless in shedding his persona until he or she is made aware of it.

Origins of Our Masks

The fundamental cause of the formation of an unconscious mask is a lack of inner security. We are afraid to acknowledge the full truth about our weaknesses, limitations, and faults. Instead, we carefully select and emphasize the good, well-developed qualities of our personality, while we ignore or deny anything that might make us unpopular or destroy others' opinion of our worth. The more we desire the good opinion and approval of peers or superiors, the more we will try to act to please them and neglect consideration of those areas of our personality which seem unimportant to others and their estimation of us. To desire others to like us is normal; but we must not seek this so intensely that we are willing to deceive them by hiding the real truth about ourselves.

The more insecure we feel and the more dependent we are upon the good opinion of others, the tighter will become the masks we wear. The longer we live this sham the more we add to our insecurity so that a vicious circle of anxiety is formed and pretense and artificiality weigh us down.

Our masks often develop when we attempt to live according to a standard that is higher than the one God has chosen for us. For example, people attempt to do more than their talents and energy can tolerate. The more impossible or difficult the goal chosen by us, the greater conflict there will be between our superficial, external conduct and our inner reality. Most of us cannot consciously live for a long period this kind of lie; so for self-protection, an unconscious wall is built between our outward conduct and our inner self. Others may see our insincerity; but we are able to live in blissful ignorance of the contradiction until some tragedy occurs or some brave soul is able to make us see the duplicity in our lives.

Egotism and selfishness are frequently responsible for our choice of a goal beyond our capabilities. The proud or vain person continually lives some false ideal. If our ideal is higher than the one destined for us, we will be filled with scruples, anxiety, fear, discouragement, and even despair at our inability to live according to this exalted goal. Difficult as these emotional disturbances are, they are healthier than the formation of a mask which lulls our inner self to sleep and allows us to be content with a mere external compliance to the false ambition we have chosen. It is impossible for a person consciously to live a lie continually; either we must find a way to establish ourselves solidly in the truth or we are forced to establish an unconscious wall between our external behavior and our inner self.

External pressure from parents, teachers, and others in authority may have been responsible originally for our choice of a wrong goal. Whenever some standard of conduct is imposed on us, one of three things will happen: open rebellion, natural acceptance, or formation of a mask.

If our personality and will are stronger than the personality of the one who attempts to tyrannize us, we will rebel against this unjust transgression of our freedom. The rebellion may be open or secret; but, as long as we are conscious of our defiance, no unconscious mask will be formed.

On the other hand, there are certain phlegmatic persons who seem to be born-followers, who need someone with a strong will to tell them what to do. If the ideal is within their capabilities, these persons can often find true happiness and authenticity; but if the ideal set for them is beyond their capacity, they will break completely beneath the load and either die or suffer a mental, emotional, or physical collapse.

When a false standard of conduct is imposed upon persons who are insecure and full of fear in the face of a superior force, there will be an outward compliance but an inner unconscious rebellion. This results in the growth of unconscious hypocrisy. They will not be aware consciously of the deceit that exists in their life, because they have developed a wall between their external agreement and their unconscious disagreement. This wall or mask is necessary for their self-protection and for the avoidance of open defiance.

Teachers who wear masks will force those under them either to conform or to rebel. Those who choose to stay under their tutelage are compelled by necessity to wear a mask also. Likewise, parents who urge their children to carry out the parents' unfulfilled dreams and ideals will cause either open rebellion or the formation of unconscious masks in the children. The greater the distance between the demand of the parent and the capability of the child, the heavier will be the mask that the child is obliged to wear between the false life it is forced to follow and the authentic image of God it was created to express.

Masks are also formed when parents and educators urge their children or pupils to follow a model of virtue exemplified in some great person. Anyone who attempts to copy exactly the life of any other human person, no matter how great or how perfect the other might have been, will find it impossible to be true to the particular melody God has destined for him or her to play.

If a parent or teacher lacks authenticity, it is quite likely he or she will try to put all the children or pupils into one mold—the particular ideal which has been pictured as being right. Woe to the independent child who refuses to adapt to this image of perfection! He or she is persecuted and considered a "bad" child in the eyes of the teacher and the other students who willingly conform. For the average child, the only way to survive a situation of this kind is to develop a mask and live a double life full of hypocritical conformity.

Teachers and parents must be careful not to demand too much of their students, and children must allow an opening for freedom at all times. Educators must be careful not to impose their will too strongly upon those under them. Students must be allowed to disagree and state opposing views. Even though this will cause a certain amount of disorder and confusion, it is less dangerous than rigid control. If fear is the predominant atmosphere in a school or home, the young people will obey externally yet secretly rebel against all that they are forced to do. For the time being they may be willing to be Pharisees in order to survive; but once they escape from the pressure and presence of their parents or teachers, those who are truly honest will revolt against everything for which their parents or teachers stand. In this way in the long run, the parents or teachers have stifled the growth and potential for love in these young people.

In these days of mass media of communication (television, slick magazines, high pressured advertising), we are unconsciously influenced by public opinion. Instead of leading our own unique life, we allow ourselves to be ruled by outward criteria, the opinions and judgments of the people who work in advertising offices or write the scripts of the movies and TV shows. Because of a constant bombardment from the media, we often unconsciously conform to what other people say or do. The anonymous, impersonal power of public opinion operates not only in the latest fad; it is also present in exaggerated conservatism: "It has always been done this way." Unconsciously we become slaves to outside influences and fail to use our ability and responsibility to think and make decisions for ourselves. Public opinion is like a cushion that stands between our person and the world. Our personal responsibility is lulled to sleep; all risk is avoided; no chances need to be taken. Instead we sink to the level of collective being, a mass product. To grow in authenticity, we must be willing to shed our dependence upon public opinion, think for ourselves, take chances, be different, be considered peculiar and unique. We must be willing to bear the brunt of criticism and even laughter.

People in professional life and especially those who must wear a uniform are particularly susceptible to the assumption of a mask. Those who have to play a particular role before others all the time are tempted to forget that this is not their real self and begin to imagine that it represents a true picture of themselves. Those who occupy high positions of authority or power for any long period of time will easily imagine that the power belongs to them by merit of their own worth rather than by merit of their position. It is almost impossible to avoid a mask and keep one's authentic self separate from the authority represented. To the degree that the one in power is selfish and egocentric, to that extent will he seek to repress the authentic image of self and try to convince himself and others that the mask he wears is the real truth.

Evil Results of Wearing A Mask

Wearing a mask affects every part of the human psyche, both the unconscious and conscious areas. The sense impressions we receive of external reality are colored so that we see only what the mask wants us to see. Anything that is contrary to the artificial role we have assumed is filtered out before it gets to our mind. Our intellect, feelings, and judgments are prejudiced by the false ego we have assumed. The mask gives such a distorted picture of reality that we become unable to make balanced judgments or right decisions about anyone or anything.

Wearing masks makes hypocrites of us. In the words of Christ to the Pharisees, we become whited sepulchers which outwardly appear beautiful to men but within are filled with rottenness. "Woe to you, Scribes and Pharisees, hypocrites, play actors that you are...you appear like good men on the outside but inside you are a mass of pretense and wickedness" (Matt. 23:13-28). No matter how prominent the role we must play in the world, no harm will result if we clearly distinguish between our official position and our authentic self. The danger of hypocrisy is present when we forget how weak and limited we personally are and try to convince ourselves that we are actually like the role we have assumed.

The masks we wear become quickly a cloak to hide and even stifle our real personality. Those who habitually wear masks will often experience that their personalities are stunted and that they are not growing into the particular fullness destined for them. A mask puts our whole personality into a strait-jacket that prevents us from expanding to our intended wholeness.

The lack of sincerity and authenticity makes us unable to find inner peace, joy, security, and fulfillment in life on earth. The falsity of our life makes us uneasy and dissatisfied. Others become unwilling to put their trust in us; they may not be able to put their finger on the reason for their distrust; but they feel that there is something unnatural or dishonest about us. Our lack of simplicity and genuineness causes people to avoid us whenever possible. At the same time, we will be suspicious of others because we project upon them our own lack of authenticity and imagine them to be as deceptive and untruthful as we unconsciously are. A person wearing a mask will experience a deep uneasiness about him/herself and others that not only destroys one's own happiness but makes it impossible for those around him/her to find complete peace and satisfaction.

Those who wear masks are unable to form true and lasting friendships with others because love is the encounter or contact of one person with another. The mask will always stand between the two persons and prevent a true encounter. If both husband and wife wear masks, they may be able to achieve a physical union; but they will not have the much more satisfying psychological and emotional union.

The same is true with our attempts at personal encounters with God. Only that part of the reality of God that is in accord with the role we have assumed is allowed to filter through into our perception of God. The liturgy no longer is an experience of love but exists on a purely neutral level as a mere duty to be performed; and our prayer life becomes lackluster, dry, and distracted and is not a dialogue of persons.

Those who continually wear masks have a tendency to seek some form of unconscious compensation in their private life. The man who is forced to wear a mask all day at work will frequently become a real bear or lion at home. The smooth, polished, and highly cultured professional may make life intolerable for his wife and children. The society wife who attempts to live beyond her capabilities is often a demon to her husband and children. Whatever of our real nature is repressed in conscious life will be expressed in some way—through anxiety, dreams and nightmares, phobias, complexes, scruples, idiosyncrasies, neuroses, irritable moods, or unreasonable outbursts of temper. Many psychosomatic illnesses of the body, mental diseases, and emotional disturbances can be traced to the unconscious masks people wear. All of these disturbances are nature's way of trying to awaken us to the realization that something is wrong in our psychic life.

Discovery and Resolution of Our Masks

The longer we have worn our masks, the more difficult it is to recognize them and rid ourselves of them. We can, therefore, be grateful if our authentic, inner self continues to wage war upon our affectations until we have happily resolved them.

To begin the task of discovering and resolving our masks, we should presume that there are still some masks which we are now wearing without being aware of them. Once we are willing to face this possibility, we try to be completely open with ourselves and others. We must find the courage to face the unpleasant facts of our life, no matter how bad and unpopular these things might be. We must urge our friends and advisers to tell us where they see us to be less than genuine, where they see or suspect some unconscious mask that is being worn by us.

To discover our masks, we must accept wholeheartedly our authentic self regardless of how limited, small, or insignificant it may seem to be. If we can be satisfied to please God and simply to measure up to his desires for us, we will find it easier to make a declaration of independence of human respect, public opinion, and the judgments of our friends. At the same time, if we can come to an appreciation of God's infinite mercy, love, goodness, and willingness to forgive, we will not be afraid to acknowledge the truth about ourselves, no matter how shameful it may seem to be. We will remember that God judges us primarily by the degree of our honesty and truthfulness.

The price of self-exposure frequently appears to be a very high one, especially if we are filled with insecurity and anxiety about ourselves. However, as soon as we are willing to expose the full truth about ourselves, we will find ourselves free of the slavery to our masks. Any external approval we might receive from others because of the masks we wear will never really satisfy us. Intuitively or instinctively we realize that this approval rests on a very shaky foundation; so we keep asking for renewed assurances. On the other hand, when we find the courage to let others know us as we really are, we will realize that any love we now receive is usually a lasting love based on truth. What a blessing it is to have a friend or counselor with whom we are not afraid to be ourselves! As long as there is at least one person with whom we can step out of uniform, "let our hair down", and be truly natural and genuine, the unconscious masks we have been wearing will begin to loosen and reveal themselves. The first step in facing the truth and resolving our masks will be the most difficult. Once we have experienced the benefits which come from shedding our masks, we will find the courage to continue this task as long as we live.

Good Results of Shedding Our Masks

To resolve our masks is like coming out of a dark cavern into the fresh morning air with the birds singing and everything expressing a delightful sense of freedom. Repressed potentialities in our character begin to reveal themselves to us. Slowly a new consciousness of ourselves and our real nature takes shape. This is the real "I"—the true center of our being which is now becoming conscious and is

97

being united with the ego. For a time we may feel somewhat uncertain and insecure in this new-found freedom. We don't know exactly how to act; but, as we progress in authenticity, we realize that we have at last discovered the truth about ourselves and are now really free for the first time in our life. Having found our true self, we can now begin to live as God intends us to live. We experience a release of oppressive tension and the liberation of spiritual energies hitherto repressed.

Other happy consequences follow our release from the slavery of our masks. We become sensitive to the needs of others and are more keenly aware of everyone and everything around us. Even physical nature takes on a fresh look. It is as though a thick, protective covering has been removed from the eyes of our soul and now we see the reality of God and God's creation. Perhaps for the first time in our life we experience a truly personal encounter of love with our brethren and with God. Prayer becomes more meaningful and during liturgical services we personally encounter both Jesus Christ and the community of our worshipping brethren.

The resolving of our masks produces a new "sixth" sense which enables us to bring about a real union of the conscious and unconscious depths of our psyche. When this happens, magnificent and unforeseen psychic energies, which give new strength to our body and increased enthusiasm and creativity to our mind and soul, are released. Life on earth really becomes worth living. We are glad to be alive and look forward with keen anticipation to each new day. Even the death of the physical body no longer holds the terror it formerly had for us. Somehow we realize that it all fits into a pattern for our good. We are relieved of our tensions and fears about the future. The inner and outer elements of our personality now live more in harmony and balance, working together as a team rather than in contradiction to each other.

CHAPTER ELEVEN

OUR SHADOWS ALWAYS FOLLOW US

The more we become identified with the masks we wear and the roles in life we must play, the more we are compelled to deny and repress those aspects of our personality that are not compatible with the character we have assumed. The more perfect we consciously imagine ourselves to be, the darker and more deeply hidden our shadow becomes. The shadow is a counterpart of our conscious ego and is the opposite of the image we would like others to think we are. The shadow is not necessarily evil but it contains those parts of our personality which are underdeveloped, primitive, childish, or unadapted to polite society. It is anything in us that we find uncouth, shameful, animal, or unbearable to accept as being a real part of ourselves. Just as everyone wears some sort of mask or persona, so everyone possesses an unconscious shadow. In fact, the two are partners in crime. The persona is the smoke screen we unconsciously throw up to hide our shadow from our consciousness.

These restrained parts of our personality may in fact be positive and creative. Frequently they are the origin of our best inspirations and the source of vitality for our life. However, since they do not fit into the particular pattern of life which we have chosen, they are rejected by our consciousness and relegated to our unconscious. There they create a more or less autonomous split in our personality which coalesces into what is called the shadow. The shadow is the "Mr. Hyde" side of our personality which we have hidden to play more easily the "Dr. Jekyll" role which we have chosen for ourselves. Because we have not given sufficient effort and attention to the proper education and training of our "Mr. Hyde" character, it will always be somewhat wild, uncivilized, uncultured, and erratic. This in turn causes us to become embarrassed whenever this side of our personality shows itself. Thus we seek more and more to hide it not only from others but even from ourselves. Because the shadow is unpleasant and difficult to handle, we prefer not even to think about it or accept ownership of it. Such repression does not cause the shadow to go away or diminish. Instead it gradually becomes stronger and more independent of our conscious will and attention. We often imagine that if we put the things of which we are ashamed out of our conscious memory, they will go away and will no longer disturb us. So we cluster around our conscious ego all those things in our personality in which we take pride or like to talk about or hear others praise.

No matter how hard or how long we have been working at the tasks of maturity and authenticity, there will always be some parts of our nature which we have not yet succeeded in bringing to the surface of consciousness. Repression is the opposite of confession, and it is the direct result of a lack of honesty and sincerity concerning ourselves. Repression is the easy way of ridding ourselves of some disagreeable decision or some embarrassing situation. Because we are ashamed, we half-consciously choose to look the other way and refuse to admit that some fault or crude habit belongs to us. Rather than accept ownership of unpleasant facts about ourselves, we try to push them out of our mind. After a time, this whole mechanism of repression takes place instantaneously without our being consciously aware of what we are doing.

The less conscious we are of this dark side of our character, the more problems it poses. Like a hurricane sucking up strength over the open waters of the ocean, the repressed shadow experiences a vigorous growth when confined exclusively to the unconscious and gradually becomes more and more threatening to our general welfare.

The more egocentric we are, the more we try to hide anything weak, inferior, shameful, or unseemly from our conscious valuation of ourselves. Fearing that we are no good, or that others will not like us, we refuse to admit anything degrading or humiliating. Most of all, in our insecurity we strive by every possible means to hide from others anything of which we think they would disapprove. Frequently, the original cause of our hiding the unpleasant parts of our personality was a lack of good experiences of love in our childhood and youth. In a loveless environment we were forced to rely entirely upon our own conscious resources; and so to protect the ego-strength needed to survive in a hostile world, we repressed everything that threatened the good image we wanted to have of ourselves. Thus we refused to accept the fact that every human being is an admixture of good and bad, positive and negative traits.

During the first 25 or 30 years of life, the egocentric person can often succeed in keeping this shadowy side of character completely hidden. However, as our conscious knowledge becomes more separated from the unconscious shadow, the ego finds it more and more difficult to control the whole personality. A certain rigidity overwhelms the conscious life so that one becomes distrustful of one's decisions and abilities. We find ourselves filled with doubts about our own worth, troubled with scrupulosity or unreasonable fears of failure, and afraid to make any kind of commitment. At times we are full of self-condemnation; at other times there is the over-compensation with exalted ideas of our worth. A real split in personality begins to show itself. Either we consciously acknowledge this schizoid character or it continues to grow beyond our control.

Discovering Our Shadow

There are a number of ways to uncover our shadow and accept those parts of our disposition which we have been repressing. For example, what are the unpleasant parts of our personality that we do not like to talk about, try to cover up, and make excuses for? What are the things that make us blush when brought to our attention, or that fills us with tears of self-pity, or that cause us to be apologetic and full of ready explanations when others remind us of them? When do we feel chagrin, embarrassment, or want the earth to open up and hide us? When do we want to run away, forget, go to bed, or wish we could die? When do we say, "I don't care, it doesn't matter" when down deep we know it matters very, very much? Where are we most reluctant to take chances and risk ourselves? What are the things that make us the angriest, or cause us to protest the most vehemently when brought to our attention? What are the unpleasant experiences that cause hives to break out, result in a bad headache or pain in the back of our neck? If we can answer these questions honestly, we will be well on the road to discovering our shadow.

Another way to discover our shadow is to study the particular faults of others that make us most angry and upset. The shadow expresses itself primarily in projection onto others. What we cannot admit in ourselves we often find in others. We become excessively disturbed with any person who happens to express outwardly the particular faults or weaknesses which we have been trying to hide. Rather than acknowledge that we possess these same faults, we find it more comfortable to direct our attention and ire to another person who seems to possess the fault. Much of the criticisms, back-biting, uncharitable gossip, and rash judgments we vent against others are actually evidence of our own repressed shadow. The more vehement and irrational our criticisms, the more clearly does the picture of our own shadow emerge. For example, those people who are most energetic in accusing others of heresy are usually the very persons who unconsciously are the most in doubt about their own faith.

Another way to discover our shadow is to study the personality of all those persons in our dreams who are of the same sex as we. Since dreams never lie, invariably those persons of the same gender in our dreams are symbolic representations of our shadow. What don't we like in the personalities of these dream figures? How do we resemble them in real life? Dreams are nature's way of revealing to us things about ourselves that otherwise we would not know.

There is still much work to be done once we succeed in acknowledging our shadow. However it is most consoling to know that we are "over the hump" once we have the insight to accept full ownership of our shadow. We would do well to realize that, by burying the shadow, we are burying some of our best talents and energies. With this realization we would be more ready to open the hidden closets within us and bring out those skeletons which we have tried so hard to hide from others and from ourselves. However, this uncovering of the shadow must not be done too quickly, because the sudden sight of our forgotten and shameful past or the ferocious appearance of these wild, repressed, unconscious energies could be so frightening that more harm than good would result. In a gradual and orderly manner, we must set to work to expose the shadow until, by the end of our life on earth, we can hope to have completed successfully our tasks of self-knowledge and authenticity.

The Resolution of Our Shadow

To attain maturity and develop our capacity for love, we must somehow find the courage to identify our personal shadow and develop its crude energies into worthwhile traits of character. At their roots the repressed sides of our personality are all good. Our task is to bring to consciousness these wild energies and train them in the ways of love. The energy behind every fault is good. It only needs to be transformed and rechanneled. For example, the energy behind a violent temper that often erupts into fits of uncontrollable anger can be rechanneled into an experience of intense personal love for God or some human being. By giving an outlet to this energy in the proper outlet of love, we will discover that there is a diminishment in the amount of energy that was formerly wasted in anger, shouting, or violence.

The intuitions which come to us unannounced are actually the work of our shadow from the positive side. Therefore, any rejection of our shadow can render our personality dull and lifeless, or destroy our creativity, spontaneity, vitality, and enthusiasm.

Our shadow is always more pleasing to God than the false image of ourselves we may now have in the conscious ego. God loves truth and honesty and has no use for hypocritical virtues. It is better to be true to our real, valid self no matter how small or how limited it might be, than to try to live falsely beyond our capabilities. We will find happiness in life only through discovering what God wants of us, and then endeavoring to follow his will, regardless of how inferior to others it might seem to be. The sooner we can discover our inner weaknesses which threaten or hinder our growth, the better chance we have of attaining the wholeness for which we were destined. Not until we have been shocked into seeing ourselves as we really are, instead of as we wish or hopefully assume we are, can we take the first step toward meeting our individual reality.

To establish the proper balance and polarity between our conscious ego and our unconscious shadow, we usually need help from others. We need this help because so often others see us better than we see ourselves. We might think that we are hiding our insecurity and selfishness from them, but often it is quite apparent. It is more satisfying in the long run to concede the unpleasant truths we already know about ourselves and to encourage others to tell us what they see in us. If we can find a friend or counselor who is willing to criticize us in a friendly, unselfish way, we have a real treasure who will be of immense help in our growth in authenticity. Even those so-called enemies of ours who find a certain, selfish satisfaction in picking us to pieces can be of invaluable assistance in uncovering our repressed shadow. We need not take literally everything they say about us, but we should try to see whatever element of truth there is in their words. If we are good listeners and not too ready to make excuses or to justify ourselves and our actions, we can gather much information about our real selves from what others say about us.

God's grace is also needed to attain the full truth about ourselves. If we pray sincerely each day to grow in self-knowledge, the providence of God will in some way send us the needed help and courage to expose to the light of day those parts of us which we have been hiding.

As the shadow grows, our egocentric fears sometimes bring on the very crisis of which we have been afraid—the total breakdown of the ego in its ability to control our life. The catastrophe in the life of the ego is often brought about by some unconscious blunder on our part. These *faux-pas* are the result of the tension created when the ego tries to live according to some false ideal or good. If the embarrassing mistake is accepted humbly, our whole life can be changed for the better. The crisis of suffering causes a breakdown of egotism and the beginning of a new life for our inner person. The ego has been forced to accept a truth which previously it had tried to ignore, forget, or repress. As the conscious knowledge of ourselves comes closer to the actual reality of what we are in the depths of our inner being, authenticity and maturity grow apace in us.

The Relation of Our Shadow to Our Capability to Love

In order to enter into a relationship of love, we must be willing to reveal everything about ourselves to the friend or beloved. Those who carry a heavy shadow are prevented from accomplishing this task of self-revelation. By resolving one's shadow the way is open to accomplish the mutual self-revelation required for any valid encounter of love and friendship.

If we have the love and encouragement of a good friend, the crisis of facing our shadow is much easier to bear. We begin to realize that if this other person still loves us despite the shadow he or she sees and admits as being a part of us, then we must not be as bad as we imagined ourselves to be. When exposed our shadow is less terrible than we previously thought. The good as well as the evil in us is due in part to outside causes and in part to our free decisions. The important thing is neither to excuse nor to condemn ourselves but rather to discover how we can put to the best possible use the energy behind the fault which has been brought to our attention. Once we are willing to accept our own shadow as well as the shadow of our beloved, we are now able to love and be loved without fear of betrayal.

What about those who do not have a good friend, counselor, or spiritual director to whom they can go for help? What about those who lack the experience of someone who truly and unselfishly loves them? There is hope for even these lonely, forlorn people, if only they can realize that behind all their fears and pains is the desire to be loved and to give themselves in love to others. God's providence does not overlook anyone, even the most abandoned person on earth. Somehow we can believe that "For those who love God, all things work together unto good" (Rom. 8:28). These pains and fears can be the very forces which break open our potential for love and allow us to progress to a higher stage of maturity. The crises that result when we confront our shadow are actually part of the whole process of growth from childhood to adulthood, from adolescence to maturity.

The desire to love and be loved is the deepest, most powerful, and most hidden element in all human actions and behavior. The hope of being part of the living and loving stream of mankind is behind the fear, hatred, and rebellion we find so often in others or in ourselves. If only we can bring ourselves to realize that the problem is the desire to love and to be loved, then there is good reason to hope that we will resolve our shadow and conquer the demons of despair and hatred. Once we recognize that the presence of unrequited love is the driving force behind our fears, hatred, and rebellion and the resulting shadow, the way is open for growth in real love and maturity.

CHAPTER TWELVE

THE ADVERSARIES WITHIN AND WITHOUT

To keep growing in love we must first learn to confront and subdue our prime enemies: The demons within us. If we succeed in challenging and conquering them we need never be afraid of the enemies from without. This is the clear teaching of Jesus: "Do not be afraid of those who kill the body but cannot kill the soul. Rather be afraid of him who is able to destroy both the soul and body in hell" (Matt. 10:28).

Who are these enemies within, the Trojan horses within our gates, that are able to destroy both our body and our soul? They are the energies we have allowed to grow wild within our personality until they threaten to take complete control of our wills and our lives: hatred, fear, sloth, envy, anger, gluttony, lust, greed, pride, vanity, mediocrity, indifference.

Most people are aware that sooner or later one must confront these inner demons, but they lack the knowledge and expertise to combat successfully the evil complexes that dwell within their psyche. These complexes act like cowardly dogs that ferociously attack in the dark but can be subdued by anyone who throws light upon them. Since they are part of God's creation, they are not intrinsically bad; rather they have been allowed to grow unattended in the garden of our soul, and thus have become overgrown, and are now a threat to the many other plants growing in our garden. They must be pruned back and brought under the control of our will, which in turn must subject itself to the higher morality of God's will. Only when these complexes are allowed to grow wild and impose themselves upon other equally important energies of our soul and upon the lives of others do they become evil.

Confronting the Adversary

The first task in confronting our inner demons is identification. We need to know what we are fighting, for our plan of attack will vary according to the particular demon we are challenging. Sometimes the problem is so obvious that it is quite easy to recognize the real nature of the complex. More often than not, however, unless we are careful, we will be led astray by the outward appearance of what is bedeviling us. Very often that which outwardly appears terrifying may actually be something good that has remained unattended in our soul castle and thus has become a part of our shadow.

A good way to identify that which is bothering us, whether it be something from our dreams or from our conscious life, is to close our eyes and try to picture in our imagination the shape of the demon. If we can imagine it either in the form of an animal or a person, male or femaile, we will be helped in this exercise. Those terrifying objects, animals, or persons which appear to us in our dreams and nightmares symbolize the neglected, repressed, or wayward energies of our psyche. Having gotten as clear a picture as is possible of the complex, the next step is to speak to it and ask its name. We can do this for any living being whether it be human in appearance, or animal, or even a plant or tree. It is like taking the whole situation to the land of fairy tale where animals, plants, trees, and even stones and mountains can talk.

This first step of recognition is extremely important for the overall success of our venture. Therefore, we should never allow the object or concept we are confronting to remain silent but insist that he/she/it speak and identify itself. If we are not satisfied with the first answer that is given, ask if it has another name and insist that it give all its names. We know from the Bible, as well as from mythology and depth psychology, that once an object has given us its name, we have a mysterious power over it and it can no longer do harm to us as when it remains hidden. Adam was told to give names to all the animals in the Garden of Eden thus symbolizing that he was to be master of all of them. Recognizing and identifying them is half the battle of conquering them and bringing them under the control of our conscious will.

The deceivers who are the most to be feared are those demons who come to us disguised as angels of light or wolves in sheep clothing. Pride is a prime example, for it usually makes its appearance in the form of some hubris, an elation or enthusiasm connected with some noteworthy success in our endeavors. Unwittingly and somewhat unconsciously we attribute the victory to ourselves instead of to God. Let St. Paul's words be an admonition: "What have you that you did not receive? If then you have received it, why do you boast as if it were not a gift?" (I Cor. 4:7). "It is God who works in you both to will and to accomplish the good that you do" (Phil. 2:13).

If this demon of pride is allowed to grow unchecked it will sooner or later lead to one or another form of megalomania as it did in the case of Jim Jones of the Jonesville tragedy in 1978 or that of Hitler in Nazi Germany. Jesus confronted three of these demons, who were disguised as angels of light, during his sojourn in the desert after his baptism. All three are examples of the abuse of power that so frequently follows the hubris of some new faculty recently received. After his baptism in the Holy Spirit, Jesus found himself possessed with extraordinary powers over nature. These faculties were to be used for the benefit of his oppressed brethren in establishing the Kingdom of God upon earth. In the desert the deceiver approached him and tempted him to use his authority to satisfy his own needs: to turn stones into bread because he was hungry; to become head of a purely earthly kingdom with all its greed and intrigue; to show off his control of nature by floating down out of the sky into the temple precincts. In each instance, Jesus recognized the deceiver, confronted him with God's word in Sacred Scripture, and exposed the true nature of the demon. The evil demons love darkness and hate light. So, once their true nature has been recognized and called by its right name, they lose most of the potentiality to do harm.

In a sense it is fortunate that we are never able to escape from our shadow or from the presence of evil within the world. If there were no evil or sin to struggle against, we would soon become content with a minimum of good; but in the presence of sin and evil, greater efforts are made to counterbalance them. We must risk an encounter with the evil forces within us and around us, even though we are not sure whether we shall conquer the evil or be conquered by it. Therefore we face the darkness that is part of every human life and confront the shadow. Our inner demons are those parts of our psyche which can lead us either to sin and evil, and their resulting counterpart guilt, or to a higher degree of love and maturity.

Evil is misdirected love and has all the power and energy of love itself. "For stern as death is love, relentless as the nether world is devotion; its flames are a blazing fire. Deep waters cannot quench love, nor floods sweep it away" (Song of Songs 8:6-7). Evil partakes of all the same qualities that love does except that these energies are directed against, instead of toward, the best interests of everyone.

The dividing line between good and evil runs right through the middle of every one of us and through the middle of all our institutions, whether they be governments, churches, or other groupings of people. There is no authentic human life without error and evil. When we deny or ignore this fact, it becomes impossible for us to deal effectively with the reality of evil because the evil does not go away but continues to build up its power until it erupts in one form or another. Unless the evil is resolved in a positive way, it will sooner or later wreck its vengeance upon us and upon others in the world around us.

If the energy of evil is misdirected love, the main work of resolving the evil in our existence will be to bring about a change of direction in the energies spent in excessive self-love, excessive love of earthly goods, and excessive attachment to bodily pleasures. These three enemies of true love are frequently referred to as the world, the flesh, and the devil. The world symbolizes immoderate attachment to money and possessions; the flesh refers to an inordinate love for pleasures of the body; the devil alludes to the pride or unrestricted love of self to the point of self-idolatry.

Sin: The Conscious Choice of Evil

The ability to love God, the world, others, and oneself in a properly balanced way is the goal of all human growth and maturity. Excessiveness in all its forms, for example, the seven deadly or capital sins, is a self-love which is not only self-destructive but also destructive of others. The sixteenth century Spanish Jesuit, Izquierdo, states: "There is only one mortal sin, which consists in placing the goal in the creature (oneself) instead of in God."

Sin is a form of evil that originates with our own perverse will, which chooses something that slows down, holds back, prevents or stops any part of the process of love or something that affects adversely any of the four steps of love: knowledge, revelation, benevolence, union. Anything that hinders the development and extension of the unlimited potential for love present in every human heart and prevents us from loving purely and fully is an evil. If this evil is deliberately and freely chosen, it is called a sin. Our sloth,

112

greed, lust, anger, envy, pride, selfishness, gluttony, fear—insofar as we knowingly and freely choose to indulge in them and thereby slow up the process of love—become the origin of most of the evil present in the world.

Sin or evil also originates from the perverse wills of other human beings, both those who are alive today and those of previous generations. The over-all inheritance of the consequences of the evil actions of previous generations would seem to be the best understanding of what is meant by original sin.

Finally, evil originates from somewhere outside this planet. This cosmic evil is called various names in the Bible: mystery of iniquity, Satan, Lucifer, evil spirits, etc.

Sin may be the act of either an individual, or of a whole group, or even of the whole of human society. Sin may have many degrees of seriousness depending upon the consequences and the extent of one's realization and freedom when making the decision. Even when ignorance, fear, confusion, or fatigue totally or partially eliminate the guilt for the sin, the evil action can still do much harm to the progress of the human race toward its goal of unity in love. Furthermore, even when a sin has been forgiven by God, after repentance of the doer, the results of the wrong behavior have a tendency to cling like a leech to a person's inner being long after the actual event. Its evil effects may continue for many years or for many generations.

Acts of selfishness, cruelty, greed, anger, and violence call forth similar acts from others. The evil of one person, especially if that person is in a position of leadership, calls into being similar evil actions on the part of those with whom he comes in contact. When a nation, or race, or culture permits the growth of some evil within its boundaries, the effects of this social sin are insidious and long lasting. Deeply rooted social sins warp and distort the human choices of the majority of individuals in a nation infected by them. One generation passes its evil to the next. These transgressions can become institutionalized in the structure of even a highly civilized culture or nation like our own. Hiroshima, Auschwitz, Vietnam, Cambodia, and a half-starving Third World are not the result of recent decisions of a few individuals within a nation. They point to a cancerous growth of selfishness, greed, ambition for power, unjust possession of the world's resources by individuals, groups, or nations to the neglect of other peoples and nations.

The effects of social sins are often clearly visible and massively atrocious. However, the process of elimination is hard to isolate and rectification of the harm caused by them is often unmanageable. The effects and the responsibilities for deeply rooted social sins are so free-floating that they infect the whole of the society. Everyone's sin becomes no one's responsibility; and as a result nations and cultures guilty of massive social sins usually collapse and disappear from history instead of instituting an effective program of reform.

When we consider personal, individual, and social sins, the problem of sin and evil becomes a truly intolerable burden. When we add to them those cosmic evils engendered by Satan, the resolution of these evils becomes well-nigh over-powering. Were it not for our faith in Jesus Christ's redemption of sin and evil, we would be totally without hope. In fact, those who do not believe in the redemptive value of Christ's life and death are hard put to find a solution to the problem of sin and evil. However, if we put our trust in Christ's power and his promises of forgiveness and redemption, we can face the existence of sin and evil within ourselves and in the world without denying them or succumbing to despair. The resolution of these evils will always be difficult but with Christ on our side, nothing is impossible. "I can do all things in him who strengthens me." (Phil. 4:13).

The Problem of Guilt

Guilt is that feeling of sadness and revulsion toward ourselves which is experienced whenever we commit a real or imagined sin. This inner depression can be just as strong in the presence of an imagined offense as in the presence of a very real sin. Because of the many past misconceptions concerning sin, some people, especially those in midlife or older, feel a great deal of false shame and guilt. Unfortunately, many psychiatrists and other counselors, in their zeal to eradicate morbid self-reproach, frequently make the mistake of discrediting all feelings of guilt in the minds of their clients. To destroy false guilt, they find it necessary to deny sin; and so Christians and other religionists find it necessary to part company with a great many modern psychologists.

Many people find it difficult to handle guilt, i.e., to admit that they have sinned. They have such a low opinion of their own personal worth and are so insecure regarding their personal goodness that they are devastated by any further accumulation of guilty feelings. Hence, in order to relieve this suffering caused by an overpowering sense of guilt, many modern philosophers, sociologists, and humanists have readily accepted the theory of determinism which asserts that life is predetermined and that human behavior is not voluntary. By taking away the benefit of human freedom to make choices, they theoretically eliminate human sin and guilt. However, if human freedom of choice is a reality, and we know and believe this, human guilt has to be accepted as valid when the abuse of this freedom stops the progress of love.

On the other hand, many Christian leaders have indeed taught in the past a stilted morality; and because of this, one can understand why many psychologists jump to the conclusion that all sin and guilt must be eliminated from the minds and convictions of people. However, a total denial of sin and guilt goes to the opposite extreme and does as much or more harm than the former erroneous attitude.

Many emotional tragedies have been caused by a false sense of guilt engendered by a faulty teaching of morality. Jung felt that the Christian religion over-emphasizes the necessity of a completely unattainable perfection and thus leaves Christians with a bad conscience and a false sense of guilt. Whenever people, especially the young or impressionable, are taught to see sin where there is no sin, or to imagine that a sinful action is much worse than it really is, we can expect to reap a harvest of emotionally disturbed or very mixed-up people. The fear, anxiety, depression, resentment, and loneliness caused by unmerited guilt are disruptive and destructive influences to one's extension of love to others and even to oneself.

Nevertheless to deny guilt when deserved simply stops up the free flow of our authenticity as it springs forth from our unconscious. As a result, the guilt will remain underground and proceed to undermine our psychic life until we become neurotically ill.

During the Nuremberg trials the Nazi war criminals maintained their innocence denying that they had any guilt. They claimed that they had to do what they did; but world opinion has not been content to accept such excuses for the horrendous crimes they perpetuated. Throughout history the men and women who have wreaked havoc on their fellow beings by all sorts of evil deeds have consistently maintained their innocence of any guilt. Those who preach determinism and lack of human freedom wittingly or unwittingly are fostering an attitude that will justify even the worst possible social and individual crimes. Every victory for determinism is a victory for evil and a defeat for love.

Whether we consider our personal sins or the sins of modern society and its institutions, the question of sin and guilt is never clear cut. At our present state of self-knowledge, we frequently cannot determine exactly how much real sin and real guilt are in our own evil actions and evil decisions. Likewise it is impossible to judge exactly the amount of sin and deserved guilt in others. Human motivation is usually quite complex and mixed, seldom purely good and seldom purely evil. For this reason Jesus counsels us in the Sermon on the Mount not to judge or condemn others. St. Paul also declares that it is impossible for him to judge himself: "The Lord is the one to judge me, so stop judging before the time of his return" (I Cor. 4:4-5).

Even if we grant all this, any mature adult who claims that there is no such thing as personal sin or guilt is betraying the truth. Our consciences, our judgments, and our experiences testify to the fact that we are free at certain moments in life to choose either good or evil. To deny human freedom is to take away the basic spirituality of our nature which makes us different from other earthly creatures and gives us our human dignity. Even when we grant that our motivation is mixed, partly conscious and partly unconscious, common sense compels us to admit that there are times when we are free and capable of making either a good choice or an evil one.

Bearing guilt becomes an acceptable human situation when we can accept the possibility of being relieved of this burden. For those who accept the revelation of the Bible this should be no problem. Throughout the Old and New Testaments there are countless assurances of God's mercy and his willingness to forgive even the most heinous human crimes, provided one repents of what has been done, strives to make restitution for any harm caused others, and resolves to change the direction of one's life toward love and wholeness. The story of Zacchaeus, the tax collector of Jericho, is a typical example of the admission of guilt and its forgiveness. "I give half my belongings, Lord, to the poor. If I have defrauded anyone in the least, I pay him back fourfold." Jesus said to him, "Today, salvation has come to this house...The Son of Man has come to search out and save what is lost" (Luke 19:8-9).

Resolving Our Sin and Guilt

The struggle against evil must begin with ourselves. There must be an honest admission of our selfishness, our anger, and resentments, our dishonesty, our unfaithfulness, our envy and jealousy, our pride and vanity. Humility and honesty are basic virtues upon which the wholeness and maturity of life must be built. Most people are afraid to face up to their personal guilt because they imagine that thereby they become unlovable and that even God will not love them. Very often the turning point in the resolution of the problem of sin and guilt is to convince ourselves that God loves us as we are—sins and all! We do not have to win God's approval and love. God will continue to love us no matter how terrible we are or how many sins we commit. The Old Testament prophets and psalmists repeatedly tell us that God is lovingly kind and faithful to his promises to love and care for us. "Can a mother forget her infant or be without tenderness for the child of her womb? Even should she forget, I will never forget you. Behold, I have written your name on the palms of my hand" (Is. 49:15-16). The Good News of Jesus Christ is that God is ready to forgive all sins. Outcasts, sinners, and prostitutes flocked to Jesus because he convinced them that, regardless of their sins, God was ready to forgive, love, and take care of them.

God's infinite power is such that he can bring good out of evil, regardless of how long our lives have been entrenched in sin. All that God asks is that we begin anew each time we fail. God is master of "making do" with whatever he finds at hand. If his original plan for us no longer fits our life, he simply reaches back into his shelf of unlimited possibilities and chooses a new plan that fits us now. God loves us so much that he does not reject us because we fail to conform to his first choice for us. He meets us wherever we happen to be and is even able to turn the evils of our past life into good. "For those who love God (here and now) all things (even our past sins) will work together unto good" (Rom. 8:28).

Besides turning to God for help when faced with our sin and guilt, we also need to go to others for help. We are tempted to feel despair if we imagine that we are totally alone in our sin and guilt. The burden of personal sin and guilt is intolerable if we try to carry it alone. We need to find a friend or friends who will help us by listening and showing sincere empathy with our situation. The organization Alcoholics Anonymous is predicated on this need of the help of fellow humans to maintain sobriety; and the twelve steps of Alcoholics Anonymous are a beautiful summary of the wisdom of Sacred Scripture and modern depth psychology in handling the problem of sin and guilt within ourselves.

1) We admit that we are powerless over a particular evil force.
2) We believe that a Power greater than ourselves can restore us to spiritual health.
3) We make a decision to turn our will and our lives over to God.
4) We make a searching and fearless moral inventory of ourselves.
5) We admit to God, ourselves, and another human being the exact nature of our wrongs.
6) We are ready to have God remove these defects of character.
7) We humbly ask Him to remove our shortcomings.
8) We make a list of all persons we have harmed and try to make amends to them.
9) We make direct amends to such people whenever possible, except when to do so would injure them or others.
10) We continue to take personal inventory and when we are wrong, promptly admit it.
11) We seek through prayer to improve our conscious contact with God, praying for a knowledge of his will and the power to carry it out.
12) Having had a spiritual awakening as a result of these steps, we try to carry this message to others and practice these principles in all our affairs.

Having experienced help from others, our next concern should be: "What can I do to help my brothers and sisters who are in need?"

The Evil of Non-Involvement

A frequent plea heard today is, "I don't want to get involved. It is none of my affair. It is not my fault, not my doing." These excuses are used by people in large cities and even small towns while crime is being committed before their very eyes. They are used by many Americans in regard to the abuse of human rights in various parts of the world; they are used by private citizens in the face of the constantly increasing tempo of militarism by our government.

Such a course of inaction is in direct violation of the progress of the human race toward solidarity and unity in love. We are responsible not only for ourselves but also, as far as we are capable, for the welfare of the whole human race. We must get involved when any of our brethren are in need. St. Paul expresses it quite well: "If anyone is weak, do I not share his weakness? If anyone is made to stumble, does my heart not blaze with indignation?" (II Cor. 11:29). Lack of sympathetic, loving involvement is the point of the story of the Good Samaritan (Luke 10:25-37). The Jewish priest and Levite were unwilling to get implicated in the plight of their fellow Jew who had fallen among robbers, so they passed quickly by on the other side of the road. Jesus roundly condemned this action of non-involvement.

Looking the other way when one's neighbor is in trouble is a denial of the commandment of love upon which the Gospel of Jesus Christ is based. As far as we are capable, we are obliged to get involved in the alleviation of the ills and troubles of the world in which we live. The more desperate the need of others and the greater the evils around us, the more responsibility we have to get involved. As our brother's keeper, we are expected to do all in our power to relieve the burdens of our brethren.

There are many ways we might help others resolve their problems of sin and evil, and each of us must discover our particular ministry in this regard. However, we probably should begin small and do what we can to help a few other individuals. The evils in the world-at-large are so numerous and so complicated that one may soon give up in despair or exhaustion if one begins by taking on the problems of the whole world. Usually the place to begin is to help a friend find the solution to his or her personal problems of sin, evil, and guilt. From there we should go on to some of the more serious problems of evil in our society.

The Evil of War

The most serious problem of evil threatening our society today is the danger of another world war between the great nations. Such a war would almost surely become a nuclear war, even if it began in a limited or non-nuclear way. Once a powerful nation has committed itself to war, its national honor will not permit defeat until it has exhausted all of its arsenal of weapons.

The danger of either an accidental or deliberate use of nuclear weapons has become progressively greater. The problem of world peace should be the number one responsibility for all of us. The situation is so overwhelming, and national opinion for greater defense to protect our national security so strong that the few voices for peace are like lone cries in a desert wilderness. In 1962 Pope John XXIII wrote (*Pacem in Terris*): "It is irrational to think that war is a proper way to obtain justice for violated rights." In 1965 Paul VI spoke to the United Nations: "No more war, war never again." In 1981 at Hiroshima John Paul II pleaded: "Let us take a solemn decision now that war will never be tolerated or sought as a means of resolving differences; let us promise our fellow human beings that we will work untiringly for disarmament and the banishing of nuclear weapons; let us replace violence and hate with confidence and caring."

121

Both in time of war and in peace the love of enemies applies to nations as well as to individuals. C. G. Jung saw the growing fears, suspicions, and hatred between nations as an example of the projection of a national shadow upon another nation. Instead of acknowledging its own faults and evil inclinations, each nation unconsciously projects these repressed faults upon any nation that poses a threat to its national security. In the face of such international projections of national shadows, what can we as individuals or small groups of concerned citizens do to resolve these shadows? Instead of throwing up our hands in despair, let us remember that every individual has a profound influence on the whole community. The more mature and loving each of us is, the greater influence for good we have on family, local community, nation, or the whole world community. Ten just men could have saved Sodom and Gomorrah.

Regardless of how little we personally may feel responsible for these threats to world peace, we are obliged to risk our lives and welfare to save the world from drowning in a sea of nuclear proliferation. Each of us must arouse and express to the fullest possible extent all of our archetypes of love: filial love, fraternal love, spousal love, agapistic love. At the same time we must not be blind to the fact that the opposite archetypes of hatred, war, violence, and destruction are also present in the heart of each of us. If we repress this second group of archetypes and refuse to accept ownership for their presence within our personality, they do not disappear, instead they gather power and energy within us like a hurricane over the open seas and then erupt suddenly. The danger is especially great now with the present situation between nations, races, cartels, and individuals. The forces of love and hate appear to be taking on gigantic proportions. For example, the magazine "Time" (March 16, 1981) reports that one of our B52 bombers "can carry more explosive power than was set off by all participants of World War II!" A single Poseidon submarine with its 224 nuclear warheads is capable of destroying every Russian city with a population of a hundred thousand.

Both the Communist and Western world think in terms of the mass man or the security of the whole nation. On both sides the power of the individual person is ignored or denied. Only the individual person, though, can bring to consciousness the twin archetypes of love and hatred and succeed in establishing a proper balance of opposites within one's personal life. Such a tension alerts us to the vast capabilities of evil present within ourselves, our nation, and other nations. Once we have acknowledged the truth of our archetypes of evil, we are in a position to take the appropriate steps to keep them under control by developing our equally powerful archetypes of love.

> "The only thing that really matters now is whether man can climb up to a higher moral level, to a higher plane of consciousness, in order to be equal to the superhuman powers which...have played into his hands. But he can make no progress with himself unless he becomes very much better acquainted with his own nature. Unfortunately, a terrifying ignorance prevails in this respect, and an equally great aversion to increasing the knowledge of his intrinsic character."

> (Jung: Answer to Job, p. 638)

As long as we are unaware or unwilling to accept ownership for the opposing archetypes of love and hatred present within our personality and our nation, we will find ourselves slaves to whatever archetype we remain blind. Love can only be practiced in a real world where the opposite pole of hatred is recognized. Virtue is only possible when we are vividly conscious of the powerful opposing forces of evil within our personal and natural character. These evils lurk beneath the surface of consciousness in every citizen of the United States, including our national leaders. Every one of us has equal power for hatred, war, and violence as we do for love, peace, and service. The more just and virtuous we imagine ourselves to be, the more danger there is that sooner or later our latent evils will erupt into consciousness. The really authentic people, for example, the great saints, have always spoken seriously

123

about how sinful they were. Jung once remarked: "Our state of war would come to an end if everybody could see his own shadow and begin the only struggle which is really worthwhile—the fight against the overwhelming power-drive in our own shadow. (BBC Broadcast, November 3, 1947). Even one person who succeeds in becoming authentic, whole, and mature in the practice of love can make a contribution to the peace and maturity of the whole world.

> "Everything now depends on man. Immense power of destruction is given into his hand, and the question is whether he can resist the will to use it and temper his will with the spirit of love and wisdom. He will hardly be capable of doing so on his own unaided resources. He needs the help of an advocate in heaven...who brings the healing and making-whole of the hitherto fragmentary man."

(Jung: Answer to Job, p. 636)

> "So much is at stake and so much depends on the psychological constitution of modern man. Is he capable of resisting the temptation to use his power for the purpose of staging a world conflagration? Is he conscious of the path he is treading and what the conclusions are that must be drawn from the present world situation and his own psychic situation? Does he know that he is on the point of losing the life-preserving myth of the inner man which Christianity has treasured up for him? Does he realize what lies in store should this catastrophe ever befall him? And finally does the individual know that he is the makeweight that tips the scales?...the individual human being, that infinitesimal unit on whom a world depends."

(Jung: The Undiscovered Self, pp. 112-113)

Our success in helping others will usually depend upon the success we ourselves have had in resolving our own sin and guilt. Others must be taught to live under the tension of opposites in their personality as well as with the tensions between themselves and others. They too must progress in the four tasks of maturity: developing a personal authenticity, discovering their significance in the plan of God, becoming transparent in their love toward other individuals, realizing their solidarity with the rest of the human race as brothers and sisters of the same Heavenly Father.

The tension between good and evil, between love and hatred, between the conscious and the unconscious, between maturity and immaturity will continue as long as we remain on earth. The resolution of these tensions will take place only by adherence to the same way of life that Jesus followed—The Way of The Cross.

CHAPTER THIRTEEN

THE MYSTERY OF THE CROSS

Since the first generation of Christians, the cross has been the primary Christian symbol. "May I never boast of anything but the cross of our Lord Jesus Christ. Through it the world has been crucified to me and I to the world" (Gal. 6:14). In the Gospels, Jesus says no one can be his follower unless one takes his/her cross and follows him (Lk. 9:23). What is the mystery of the cross? What does it symbolize?

For Jung a symbol "represents the best expression obtainable at the time for something that is essentially unknown." If we look at the two bars which form the cross, we can think of them as expressing a two-fold tension between God and mankind and between good and evil. They also symbolize all the other tensions in the life of a fully mature, balanced Christian.

The oft-repeated theme of this book has been that love, wholeness, maturity, or sanctity become authentic, active, and growing in the presence of an ever-increasing tension between opposite poles. The cross expresses the mysterious necessity of the conjunction of opposites in all existence. All forms of energy, including psychic and spiritual, originate as a result of this interaction between opposites. The cross is the symbol which best expresses the union of opposites that must occur in any healthy, mature life and existence. The cross is a very positive symbol when we consider the new life that results from it. Without the cross there can be no growth in love or maturity, no wholeness and balance, no life and energy, no personal relationship between God and mankind.

The cross also signifies struggle, conflict, suffering, even death itself. The crucifixion of Jesus was the supreme expression of God's love for us. Our expression of love for God and others entails a similar crucifixion. "I solemnly assure you, unless a grain of wheat falls to the earth and dies, it remains just a grain of wheat. But if it dies, it produces much fruit. The man who loves his life loses it, while the man who hates his life in this world preserves it to life eternal" (John 12:24-25). The reconciliation of opposites always involves suffering and struggle but the tension results in a new psychic or spiritual energy. Sometimes only death will relieve us of the pain; but even then, if we believe Christ's promises, a resurrected life will be ours.

Evil has such a grasp on the world and on us that only through suffering, willingly and lovingly accepted, can we cause it to release its death-like grip. If people today will follow the example of Jesus Christ and experience the clash of opposites in their own life, then there is hope that our modern world will be able to avoid a terrible catastrophe which might throw back the progress of humanity thousands of years. It would seem that the time is comparatively short for us to avert such a disaster which could destroy all that has been built by many previous centuries of civilization. Only Christianity has a viable solution to the problem of evil. The Asian religions, for the most part, regard good and evil as merely varying degrees of the same reality. The Oriental sees both good and evil as illusions and seeks to be liberated from them by a state of nirvana. Western civilization with its Christian heritage, though, recognizes and acknowledges the difference between good and evil and the necessity of man to cope with it. The Paschal Mystery of Jesus' crucifixion, death, and resurrection gives us our symbols of hope.

The Christian solution does not consist of a naïve denial of the reality of evil but rather in maintaining a constant tension between the good and evil within ourselves and within the world. We should accept the fact that we will never totally eliminate our shadow and never completely destroy the evil around us. Instead of pursuing the chimera of an earthly perfection totally free of sin and guilt, we need to accept patiently and seriously the schizoid nature of our own and others' personalities. The split between good and evil in our personality will continue throughout our life on earth. The primary cross we all must carry is living constantly under this very tension of good and evil and the knowledge that it is part of human existence. Yet, this tension is not bad but good since out of the conflict of opposites comes the *elan vital*, the energy of life itself. Without the challenge that the presence of evil constantly presents us, we would soon become psychologically and spiritually dead.

The Cross, then, is the key to the whole of human history as well as to the history of each individual. At the same time, we must realize that the suffering symbolized by the cross is not in itself the goal of life but only a means to the authentic practice of a Christ-like love. God himself has gone ahead of us in the person of Jesus and has given us the supreme example of a willingness to sacrifice self for the sake of others. Jesus solved the problem of evil by entering into the very heart of evil, not as a doer of evil but as the victim of the evil forces on earth. Jesus willingly endured crucifixion and death at the hands of these evil forces. By the power of his totally unselfish love, he succeeded in redirecting the energies of evil away from death and toward a new resurrection of life at a much higher level. Something similar happens to each of us when we willingly and lovingly accept the crosses in our life. Conflict, tension, struggle, suffering, if accepted with the same disposition as manifested in the life of Jesus and in the lives of the saints, are not bad but good. Without them our life can degenerate into a dull and listless mediocrity or a vain flight into a never-satisfying round of meaningless pleasure.

128

THE MYSTERY OF THE CROSS

For many people the particular situation in which they are living is often an abundant source of suffering. Some of the uninvited crosses which they experience are: having to live with a difficult spouse; working at an unpleasant, uninspiring and difficult job; having to contend with children who have rejected the values the parents tried to instill in them; rejection by someone who used to be a friend; loss of physical or mental health; misunderstanding or misinterpretation of our motives; opposition, persecution; senility, old age and its subsequent loss of energy and memory; failure in business or other projects upon which one has spent much time, effort, and resources. Our attitude in these situations can be transformed through acceptance and love and can become a spring-board for our passage to a higher existence of fulfillment and wholeness.

Even if we make mistakes concerning God's will for us or the crosses we have chosen to carry, our life can still be a success if we live it with love and integrity. Jesus Christ, during his agony in the Garden and still more when he experienced the sense of abandonment by his Father while he was on the cross, came to the realization that for the most part his public life had been a failure. This realization probably caused Jesus much greater suffering than the physical pain of being nailed to the cross. Nevertheless he lived his life with such great honesty, virtue, and love that he still won the victory over evil through his death and resurrection.

The cross is the necessary lot of a sinful human race with deeply ingrained habits of selfishness and violence. The long history of mankind's repeated choices of wrong goals for the energies of love has created evil habits in the very fabric of our nature. Frequently we see jealousy and selfishness manifested in the actions of infants and very small children long before they are capable of making a free decision. Many human beings are so mired in these deep-seated habits that they cannot extricate themselves. Others, who have made some progress in overcoming evil habits, must come to their rescue following the pattern of Jesus' passion and death. We should offer ourselves in selfless love to help them carry their burden of evil, which alone they are unable to lift. "Even now I find my joy in the suffering I endure for you. In my own flesh I fill up what is lacking in the sufferings of Christ for the sake of his body, the Church" (Col. 1:24). If our present generation or any future generation is to be healed of its fatal propensity to violence, war and hatred; to cruelty and torture; to greed, injustice, and dishonesty; to selfishness, envy, and gluttony; to fear and oppression, there is need of a host of unselfish persons who are willing to offer themselves in a sacrifice of love.

In practical terms, what does this mean? It means to follow the path of non-violence in the face of injustice. It means to follow the example of St. Paul who tells the Corinthians: "I will gladly spend myself and be spent for your sakes, even though in loving you the more, I be loved the less" (II Cor. 12:15). It means to accept literally the teaching of the Sermon on the Mount: "Blessed are you when they insult you and persecute you and utter every kind of slander against you because of me. Be glad and rejoice, for your reward is great in heaven" (Matt. 5:12). It means to turn the other cheek, to go the extra mile, to give away our shirt as well as our cloak (Matt. 5:38-42). It means to love our enemies, do good to those who hate us, bless those who curse us, pray for those who maltreat us (Luke 6:27-28). It means to practice love to the fullest extent of our capabilities.

Sin and evil can be resolved only from within and not from without. Victim souls are those who are willing to allow the evil forces around them to afflict them yet all the time returning good for evil. To take upon oneself this role of victim without a truly unselfish love and without some sign that it is God's will could be masochistic and dehumanizing because we may find ourselves enjoying the role of being persecuted and indulge in self-pity and condescension or hatred toward those who persecute us. Only by a special grace of God are victims of persecution and victims of love able to turn the other cheek and sincerely love and pray for the persecutors. But let us not be too quick to say that we lack this special grace! In our time, Martin Luther King, Jr., and Mahatma Gandhi have given us excellent examples of what the teachings of the New Testament involve when we freely choose to become victim souls for the salvation of our brethren.

One of the greatest abuses of love is the abuse of power and authority that one human has over other human beings. Authority and obedience are the necessary complements of any well-organized and efficient gathering of human beings. However, because of the elation that the exercise of such authority begets in the human heart, there is a tendency for those possessing power to increase and hold it far beyond what is necessary for the well-being of the group. This is applicable not only to appointed or elected officials of civil government and church but also to parents, teachers, counselors, and even friends! To counterbalance abuses of power, there is the need of some human beings to follow the example of Jesus in emptying themselves of all power. The Greek word for "emptying" used by St. Paul, *kenosis*, has become popular in recent decades to describe this particular form of the cross that is so much needed in modern society where there are so many abuses of power. To counteract these abuses, the world needs victim souls willing to empty themselves of power over their fellow human beings and see themselves as servants. "Have this mind in you which was also in Christ. Though he was by nature God, he did not deem equality with God something to be grasped at. Rather, he emptied (*ekenosen*) himself and took the form of a slave" (Phil. 2:5-7).

Suffering is the price we must pay for the capability to love others unselfishly. We suffer in our struggle to overcome our inclinations to self-indulgence, our habit of putting our will and desires ahead of God's will and the welfare of others. We must go at cross-purposes to ingrained habits of evil in our personality. This task is never easy since it means doing the opposite of what we want to do, choosing minimum pleasure over maximum pleasure.

Our innate tendency is to think first of ourselves and take care of ourselves without regard for others. To reverse this inborn instinct for self-preservation and replace it with the sacrifice of self for the sake of others is onerous. Love of self must be reined in and brought under control since it is normally inclined to crowd out the love of God and love of neighbor, and in that way becomes destructive rather than constructive. However, we must not totally kill self-love; rather it must be brought into a proper balance and tension with love of God and neighbor.

Unfortunately very few people appreciate the value of suffering. Instead, they seek every possible means to escape from it. But, if we develop the habit of always running away from pain, we will miss many opportunities to overcome our egotism and sublimate life's energies into a truly worthwhile unselfish love. Rather than seek the greatest possible delight, we frequently need to sacrifice bodily and emotional gratification to make room for the life of love to grow. At the same time, we must keep a proper balance in our attitude toward pleasure so that we can give ourselves wholeheartedly to its enjoyment whenever it seems right and best to do so; but because to become enslaved to the pursuit of pleasure is so easy, we should not linger too long in it but deny ourselves in some way every day.

"If anyone wishes to come after me, let him deny himself, take up his cross daily and follow me. For he who would save his life will lose it, but he who loses his life for my sake, will save it" (Luke 9:23-24).

CHAPTER FOURTEEN

THE PRICE OF LOVE

Of all the key moments that occur during our lifetime, those that strike the closest to home, cause the most suffering, and present the most problems are the crises in the extension of friendship and love to others. Success or failure in developing wholeness is dependent to a large extent on our response in personal encounters where a loving approach or loving service is indicated. So necessary are these crises for our growth in wholeness that, if our life continues for even a few years without some sort of critical point in this area, we can be reasonably certain that our growth toward maturity has come to a dead stop or is not progressing as it should. We should not deliberately look for conflicts or make unnecessary trouble for ourselves but rather keep ourselves open to every possible encounter with our fellow human beings. If this openness is present, we will not wait long before we find some challenge facing us. Throughout our life our attitude should never be to run away from the situation and the suffering it might entail but, rather, to gird ourselves with whatever helps and strength we can find and bravely face it.

The ability to love is the most wonderful, beautiful, and satisfying power which God and man possess. Love is the life which binds the Father, Son, and Holy Spirit together in the Blessed Trinity. If we understood love in all its fullness, we would understand all there is to know about God himself. The marvel of all marvels is the fact that God has freely chosen to share with us this divine gift of love. Not only does he make us recipients of his love, but he also wills that we should love others as he loves us. "A new commandment I give you, that you love one another; that as I have loved you, you also ought to love one another" (John13:34). In no other activity does mankind participate so fully in God's work and in God's interior life as when engaged in a loving act. "Love is from God and everyone who loves is born of God and knows God. He who does not love, does not know God for God is love" (I John 4:7-8).

By love God has placed us in the center of his existence so that all his divine energies are dedicated to our welfare and happiness. By love we are supposed to place God, God's will, and the welfare of others in the center of our life and dedicate all of our energies to pleasing God and neighbor. God calls us to a life of perfect love. In the person of Jesus Christ we are able to see what this perfection of love means. "I always do the things that are pleasing to him" (John 8:29). Jesus gave his whole life to loving and serving God and his brethren. "The Son of Man has not come to be served but to serve and give his life as a ransom for many" (Matt. 20:28).

To love properly and unselfishly is seldom easy. If done successfully, it brings satisfaction and happiness but also suffering and pain. There is nothing soft or sentimental about real love; it involves stress, tension, struggle, hard work, and sacrifice. To love rightly there must be an inner conversion of our whole being away from self-indulgence and toward an unselfish giving of self to others. Love means the placing of our life and service at the feet of another person. Love requires self-discipline, which in turn is purchased only at the price of self-denial.

If we wish to love as Jesus loved, there must be a willingness to sacrifice our life and everything in it for the sake of God and the people of God. In reality, we should be willing to make such a total sacrifice of our life and being only to the person of God himself. However, since God dwells within the hearts of our brethren, we can give our life to others as Christ did for us. "Greater love than this no one has, that one lay down his life for his friends" (John 15:13).

Friendship is an act of love in which there is the free and mutual exchange of the gift of self between two or more persons. To attain this love called friendship both persons must be sufficiently in command of their inner being to be able to reach out altruistically to another person. Only mature people have enough control of their personality to make this complete gift of self; and only a balanced person is uninhibited enough to receive in a principled manner the friendship offered by another. The more adult the participants in a friendship are, the more capable they will be of fulfilling the four tasks of love: knowledge of self and the other; self-revelation; benevolence toward one another; the union of persons.

In an authentic personal encounter between two persons, whether they be God and oneself, or oneself and another human being, these four distinct tasks or elements can be discerned. We first became aware that we are drawn to know more about this particular person and in turn we want to tell them all we can of our self. We aspire to do everything we can to please them, and we yearn to spend as much time as possible in their company. Whenever these four dispositions are present in both parties, we have that situation of friendship or love so desired by everyone.

The price of learning the art of loving is the life-long struggle necessary to overcome self-centeredness in our life. If we are wrapped up in our own narcissistic interest, we will never be able to see clearly the reality of another person. Our masks and our shadow will constantly interfere with any true insight into others. Instead of being able to know the person as he or she really is, we will constantly project our own unconscious repressions upon the other and imagine that this is the reality we are loving or hating.

Self-revelation is essential to any real encounter of love. If we have centered our life in our ego rather than in God, we will find ourselves so filled with insecurity and diffidence that we will be unable to open ourselves to others and reveal the true state of our being. If we lack a sufficient appreciation of our inner worth, we will live in constant fear of being revealed as someone of no value before God and man. This inferiority complex of immature and egocentric people is a constant obstacle to their ability to real relationships of love with others. Only by conquering egocentricity and finding faith and hope in God, can we form true and lasting friendships with others.

The more egocentric and insecure we are, the more easily we are enslaved by others, especially if they are also egocentric. In the vulnerability of our self-centeredness, we will cling like a vine to the person whom we feel we need to complete our being. If the person whose love we desire is an egoist, our enslavement to him/her will flatter him/her and help to ease some of his/her own deep feelings of insecurity. Rather than being dominated by or dominating another, mature persons give and receive a free gift of self. They appreciate very much the tremendous value of loving and being loved; but they also prize their own freedom and independence. They know that it is only the truly free person who can take hold of his/her life and, without compulsion or necessity, make a real gift of it to another. The right to give our inner being is the most precious privilege that God has entrusted to us. If we fail to respect this right in ourselves or in others, we do great harm.

A person filled with egotism cannot attain that benevolence of kindness necessary for great friendship. Egocentric persons have the tendency to treat other people, even those they love, as things rather than persons. Selfish people use their friends to satisfy their own pleasure and needs, rather than go out to them in unselfish service. They become possessive or attempt to manipulate the other person to live up to their selfish expectations. Instead of being genuinely interested in furthering the welfare and well-being of the other person, the egotist tries to make another fit into the particular mold that best suits himself.

Facility in loving and forming friendships comes after years in the pursuit of maturity. Even when we find someone attractive and lovable, the road to a complete friendship is nearly always a rocky one. The union of two different persons with their diverse desires, talents, temperaments, experience, and background requires sacrifice and understanding on the part of both. The longer we have been isolated in our little world of self, the more difficult it will be to enter into the real union of souls, hearts, and wills required for friendship. In the loneliness of our immaturity and selfishness we stand off from others and imagine them to be our rivals rather than partners. Only after many years of denial of self are we able to practice true love and reach a full and real friendship with others.

The fault of egotism must be expelled slowly from our life; otherwise we may cause a complete break-down of our ego or leave a gap in the protective armor of our being. We must give ample time for the scars created by selfishness to heal and for a new growth in selflessness to mature. For everything negative that we seek to eliminate from our personality, we must find a positive and constructive counterpart to replace it. In our struggle toward maturity, if we leave a vacuum in our character we might very well experience a new influx of evil (Cf. Matt. 12:43-45).

Selfishness and egotism can do great harm by preventing love from ever arising. They can seriously injure a friendship that has progressed toward some degree of union. If one or both persons allow pride and self-love to dominate their attitudes and decisions toward the other, deep wounds and much pain will result, both for the injured party as well as for the one who is responsible for the injury. Frequently it is impossible to determine which person is the most to blame. Rather than trying to fix the exact cause of the rupture in the friendship, both should address themselves to the task of repairing the break. Otherwise the friendship will not continue.

Wounds caused by the abuse of love will usually take a long time to heal. To escape this penalty of a long convalescence is impossible; therefore, if both parties are interested in preserving and restoring the lost love, heroic efforts must be made. Not only must the guilty one do all in his or her power to repent and repair the harm caused by the failure to love, but often, and most important, the injured party too must be willing to forgive and labor to restore the love and friendship. If either the injured or injuring person chooses not to pay the high price required to repair a broken friendship, it is impossible to restore a love once it has been abused.

Every sin is an abuse of friendship that exists between God and a human soul. If we have deliberately abused God's love, we have no strict right in justice to be forgiven. But thanks to the infinite mercy of God, we know that he is always willing to restore the friendship which we have lost by our sins. However, we must not take this forgiveness for granted or use it as an excuse to keep sinning. If we have ill-used God's love or the friendship of another human being, we must be willing to follow the long, hard road which leads back to a restoration of the union that formerly existed. It is never easy to repair the deep injuries caused by selfishness and pride; but it is, likewise, never impossible, provided the other person is willing to forgive and to suffer along with us.

To grasp the art of love is never easy, for it must be relearned again and again throughout the course of our life. Let us never imagine that we have arrived at the full perfection of love. Even though occasionally we may reach a peak in the practice of love, it is normal to fall back into old habits of selfishness. Despite many beautiful moments of loving encounter with friends, the goal of perfect love and union with the beloved is attained only after a lifetime of valiant effort. No matter how well we might have loved yesterday, there are still higher pinnacles of love to be reached today and tomorrow. Like mountain climbers, we should arise each morning with the determination to climb still another unscaled peak or unexplored area of love. The territory of love is so vast that we will never finish the tasks of love no matter how long we live.

Always we must strive to give more love than we receive. First of all, this is our way of showing gratitude to God and other benefactors for the love we have received from them. Secondly, people can learn love only from a personal experience of someone loving them. If we succeed in furnishing even one good experience of love to another, that person may be convinced to the value of love and be converted to a lifetime of loving service to others. To teach love by words is impossible; only by mature, unselfish acts will love be taught.

Whenever we allow ourselves to become wrapped up in our selfishness, we slow down the whole process of maturation and unification of mankind in God and in love. If we desire to do our part in the work of God on earth, we must be willing to sacrifice our own momentary advantage and show true concern to everyone who comes within our sphere of influence. No sacrifice is too great to help Jesus Christ establish his reign of love upon earth. Jesus has done his part by becoming man and dying for us on the cross. It is now our task to take up the cross of self-denial and by the heroic practice of pure love to carry on Christ's work of salvation upon earth.

CHAPTER FIFTEEN

PERSONAL FRIENDSHIPS

Our inner self or person is so created that it cannot be complete when it stands alone, apart from other persons. Only when our person is joined in love to another person or persons can we experience those tremendous releases of energy, life, enthusiasm, and creativity which are the happy lot of anyone who has had a real encounter of personal love. The human seems to be possessed with an unlimited potential of life, goodness, love, and happiness. Each encounter of love with another person, be they human or divine, releases a new outpouring of these wonderful treasures. The fullness of our capacity for love and happiness can be attained only in that greatest of all encounters between our person and the person of God. If we are successful in reaching this union of love with God, we will have accomplished the deepest desire of our inner being and will experience fulfillment. However, God does not dwell in heaven alone but exists in a special way in the hearts of all human beings. Hence, it is usually impossible to have a complete love of God until we succeed in entering into personal encounters of love with other human beings.

Since each person is absolutely unique in the particular way he or she reflects in the image of God, every personal relationship offers something new and different. The more experience we have in giving and receiving love, the more we realize that there is something of the greatness and power of God in each new encounter. The joy of each new friend must be akin to the joy that God experienced when he first created man and placed him in a garden of delight. The newness and uniqueness of each friendship is like the freshness of the early morning of a bright, new day. We can remember other days that were similar to this present one; but each new day, each new creation, each new friendship has a delight and satisfaction all its own. We cannot compare one love or friendship with another, because each is so distinct and unusual that it stands alone on its own merits.

To know the delights and satisfactions of love on earth, it is not enough to love people in general; we must make the necessary effort to love individual persons and give them the same respect and attention we give ourselves. Our potentiality for love is capable of unlimited expansion, and the maturation of our person depends on the development of our ability to form personal friendships. In the life we hope to live with God after death we will find this capability for love developed to the highest possible degree. Heaven is not only sharing the same personal life of love which the Father, Son, and Holy Spirit share; it is also entering into the deepest possible personal friendship with every other individual who has ever lived and is with God. In a most special way, we can hope to renew in heaven those personal friendships which have meant so much to us upon earth. Actually, we will be able to enter into an immensely deeper encounter of love than we ever succeeded in attaining upon earth. However, the more unselfish our earthly love for others has been, the more beautiful will these same friendships be when we meet each other in heaven. No longer will we suffer the limitations of earth, but without any inhibitions we will be able to surrender our whole being to the joy of loving.

To the extent that we have succeeded in purifying our souls of selfishness and have been able to exercise our faculties of giving and receiving pure love, to that extent we are already in heaven, while still on earth. St. Teresa of Avila once remarked: "All the way to heaven should be heaven too." Ideally, we should not have to wait until after death to experience pure, unselfish love. If we are sufficiently unselfish, we can have many beautiful, heaven-like experiences of love upon earth. We were created to love and be loved; every other task on earth has meaning only when it aids in developing our powers for unselfish, mature love.

At times we may be tempted to imagine that the effort required for maturity is too great. Once we realize, though, the essential connection between the degree of our wholeness and our competency in loving, we are more inclined to pay the high price of unselfishness necessary for growth in maturity. The more we try to love others in a personal way, the more we should realize the need of becoming authentic, unselfish, pure, and whole in all areas of our psychic life. It is impossible to love another person or to receive a personal love from another as long as we are engrossed in our own selfish desires. We must be willing to lose ourselves and give ourselves to others as totally and completely as possible; otherwise, our love is not sincere and pure.

We may have to wait until old age to experience the perfection of unselfish loving. However, it is worth the countless sacrifices of early life and middle age to be able, even in our old age, to taste something of the joys of pure, ungrudging giving and receiving of love.

If we have been blessed with parents, teachers, friends, and benefactors who have given us an unstinting love, we should even now be well along in the development of our capability for loving. Having received so much love from others, we now have the obligation to give ourselves wholeheartedly to loving everyone. However, even if we were deprived of good experiences of love in the past, we must not feel sorry for our unhappy lot. Let us accept our situation as we find it and make the most of whatever opportunities for love that are now presented. We learn to love by exercising to the fullest possible extent all our faculties for love. Even the most neglected and forlorn person has some ability to love. Although this love may be imperfect, it is still better to love in this way than not to love at all.

Once we realize the value and importance of personal friendships, we will strive for that genuineness and sincerity which must be present in our hearts if we wish others to trust us in our efforts to love them. Full of determination to learn the art of personal love, we will tear away the masks which prevent our knowing ourselves as we really are; we will take hold of our unconscious shadow and try to convert its powers into the energy of love; we will practice self-denial and self-discipline so that we can make a true gift of ourselves to others. The more we experience love, the more unafraid we will be to open our hearts in love to others. Even though we may find ourselves rebuffed and our offers of friendship refused, we will persist in going out to others with the gift of self in love.

If the proper order and balance are kept in our love, experiences of personal friendship with other human beings will in no way interfere with the possibility of our friendship with God. No human person will ever be placed ahead of God or loved more than God; human love will never be allowed to destroy our union with God or cause us to disobey God's will and commandments. However, it would be a total contradiction of God's goodness and wisdom to imagine that he would give us other human persons who are so lovable and attractive and yet forbid us to love these same persons. As long as we succeed in keeping the right order in our love as shown us by common sense, divine revelation, and the wisdom and experience of the ages, we should never be afraid of human love and personal friendships.

Ordinarily, it is impossible to have satisfying encounters of love with God without previous encounters of love with other human beings. These experiences of human love should not only be love received, such as love of parents, teachers, or friends, but ordinarily we must also have felt real love for other human beings before we can feel the fullness of a personal encounter with God. Very often, people are dry and distracted in their relationship with God and feel no devotion in prayer because they have lacked good, satisfying experiences of parental, filial, or spousal love in their life. There are exceptions to this. But normally the growth in our realization of the love of God, which we call grace-life, is directly proportionate to the progress we have made in the area of personal love and friendships with other human beings. When we stop progressing in purity, unselfishness, and maturity in our human encounters of love, our whole relationship with God invariably suffers a serious regression or at least apathy and aridity.

In order to have a personal encounter of love with another person, be it divine or human, we must be able to make direct contact with the other person. We must see the other as a real being with the same rights, privileges, and value as ourselves. Of course, if we consider ourselves worthless, we will be unable to respect the merit of another and will be incapable of achieving the personal union necessary for love. Without the freedom and self-possession habitually seen in mature people, it is not possible to make the free and total gift required for a perfect encounter of love. Freedom and maturity should be present in both the person who gives the love as well as in the person who receives it; otherwise, the equality required for a real friendship will be lacking. This is true even in our encounters of love with God. By sanctifying grace we have been elevated to a certain equality with God so that we share the same life as do the three persons of the Blessed Trinity. Because the Second Person, Jesus Christ, has stooped to our level and made himself one with us, it is often easier to enter into a personal encounter with Jesus than with God the Father or the Holy Spirit. Since he is so much like us, we can go to Jesus without fear or hesitation and open our hearts in love to him.

Despite the prerequisite of self-possession of maturity for perfect love, it would be a mistake to wait until we are completely mature before attempting to give ourselves to another in love. Nor must we wait until we find another absolutely mature person before extending our offer of friendship. The growth of love and maturity are mutually dependent upon each other. We learn to love as we become more mature, and we mature with every new experience of love. Even though our present friendships may still be imperfect, we should cultivate as many of them as possible. In each we must try to purify our gift of self. Instead of lingering in selfish pleasure or thinking only of what we hope to receive from the friendship, let us try to forget our own wants and needs and give ourselves, our time, and our talents to helping the other. Let us take each other as we are, with all our imperfections and present selfishness, and endeavor to take another step forward toward the perfection of love.

No matter how beautiful or enjoyable any present friendship might be, many years of self-effacement are still necessary before this encounter of love will reach its fullest possible perfection. The four tasks of knowledge, self-revelation, benevolence, and union require continual and resolute efforts on the part of both persons before the final goal of perfect love is attained. God in his mercy frequently allows two friends to taste something of the total happiness of perfect love when they first experience an encounter of love. Without this first taste of the joys of love, it is doubtful that many people would find the courage and perseverance to carry out the difficult tasks of a mature friendship. In the years of sacrifice that follow the first awareness of love, the persons involved may be tempted many times to imagine that their first impressions were wrong and that love or friendship is not worth all the effort. However, these trials and temptations are the real tests of a valid and unselfish love. If they are endured, wonderful experiences of pure love and devoted friendship are in store for us.

Differences of temperament between two individuals can often be the source of disharmony or friction and unhappiness. We have a tendency to imagine that others react, think, feel, judge, and act the same way we do, or at least they should do so. When they do not, we fail to comprehend the reason for their peculiar actions and reactions. A knowledge of the different temperaments would help toward the solution of many of the misunderstandings and disagreements that arise in almost every personal friendship.

Not all growth in love is dark and full of suffering or sacrifice. Many happy moments of peaceful love can be expected in every worthwhile friendship. Each of these encounters is like a preview of what can be expected in the future, if both are willing and able to persevere in their efforts and purify themselves and pay the price required for perfect love. If a friendship is to grow and mature as it should, both persons must reconcile themselves to the fact that, upon earth, they must always carry the cross of self-sacrifice and follow Christ on the road to Calvary. Our Calvary is the crucifixion of our egocentricity and selfishness. After each sacrifice, if we keep struggling, we will experience a new resurrection to a higher level of maturity and a more wonderful relationship of love than ever previously enjoyed. However, until our final death and resurrection in heaven, we must continue to suffer and die to ourselves in order that we may rise to ever newer and higher levels of Christian love.

CHAPTER SIXTEEN

MALE/FEMALE RELATIONSHIPS

Of all the personal friendships possible upon earth, the one between a man and a woman most closely resembles the love that exists in heaven between the Father, Son, and Holy Spirit. Parental love and fraternal friendship can be most satisfying and enjoyable; but seldom do they reach the peak of fulfillment that can be found in a truly unselfish love between two persons of the opposite sex. On the other hand, there are countless marriages and other relationships of love between men and women which fall far short of the ideal spousal love which might be possible and which almost everyone hopes to attain sometime during life on earth. An ideal friendship is not something ready-made and bestowed upon every man and woman who happen to fall in love with each other. It is the fruit of many, many years of developing understanding, patient empathy, and real consideration for the other.

What are some of the problems that make the fulfillment of love between a man and woman so difficult? First, in any encounter of love between two people of a different sex, the most powerful of all human passions is aroused. The natural, physical and spiritual attraction between a man and a woman is highly explosive; therefore, safeguards must be present to protect the integrity of this love and to prevent it from doing more harm than good.

These precautions would be necessary in any culture, but they are especially needed in our present Western culture where we find two extreme attitudes toward sex. One extreme—the Puritan, Jansenistic, or Platonic attitude— considers the body, the flesh, and all the pleasures of the flesh as somewhat evil or at least less good than the things of the spirit. The other extreme—pagan, free love— considers the pleasure of the body, and especially sexual pleasure, as having no law of limitation or prohibition. All who live in today's world are somewhat contaminated, either consciously or unconsciously, by one or both of these attitudes of prudery or prurience.

A second problem that frequently arises is "unrequited love." It is always possible that a person will be drawn to someone without that other person feeling any mutual attraction. This risk of rejection is present in every offer of friendship made to another person, but especially is it possible in relationships between men and women. Great suffering results when our love is rebuffed, but we must take this chance or no encounter will ever occur. Freedom is so absolutely essential to every relationship of love that we can never force friendship upon someone who does not want it. Justice can be demanded of another, but love can only be wooed. If it is given, it will always be a free gift which no one ever deserved in the strict sense or should expect as a matter of course. Actually, the free consent of three different persons is required before a human encounter of love is possible. Not only must both human persons freely and fully desire and agree to give themselves in love to each other; God and destiny must also give their consent through the many diverse elements of divine providence which must coalesce to create any lasting friendship.

Difficult as the first two problems might be, there is another that is more serious. What is to be done when a husband or wife falls in love with someone other than the one to whom he or she is married? The problem cannot be answered by saying that this must never be allowed to happen. Since we are constantly meeting people of the opposite sex, it can be safely presumed that sooner or later everyone will have the experience of being drawn to a person other than the one to whom one is married. Such a situation is fraught with complexities for everyone concerned. Without great care a terrible tragedy can, and frequently does, occur. Besides the obvious problems of jealousy and unrequited love, human nature is so created that every deep love between a man and a women sooner or later, consciously or unconsciously, desires to be completed through physical union. When this possibility is denied, only a heroic and selfless person can survive the deep and strong feelings present in every situation of unsatisfied love. It would be a rare exception to find a purely platonic friendship between a man and a woman; either consciously or unconsciously the sexual attraction will be present if the friendship is allowed to continue for any length of time. What, therefore, are the guidelines to be followed to prevent the tragedy of adultery, divorce, broken home, or abandoned vocation?

Because any real friendship requires the total giving of self to each other, the ideal friendship between persons of the opposite sex is seldom possible, except in marriage, or at least in a situation where legitimate marriage is possible in the foreseeable future. At our present level of maturity, in practical life, it would seem that few people are capable of a total and permanent spousal love apart from marriage. Anyone who would dare to consider himself or herself an exception to the rule should use great care and every precaution to prevent self-deception or the involvement of oneself and others in a tragic situation that could cause great harm to many persons. In our observations of the current trend among young people to live with each other without marriage, we note that many of them eventually do enter a legal, contractual marriage. This seems to indicate that, to survive, spousal love needs commitment, public sanction, and stability in addition to mutual attraction.

Probably the most important of the safeguards needed in any encounter of love between a man and woman is an objective friend, counselor, or spiritual director. When dealing with erotic love, one's own judgments can scarcely be trusted because reason and conscience are easily blinded by passion and desire. To benefit from the help of this third person, one must be absolutely honest, completely open, and sincere in revealing to the counselor one's deepest feelings, most secret thoughts, and desires. To be effective, the counselor should be wise, experienced, and sufficiently detached from the situation so that he or she can make objective judgments and give advice without projecting his or her own unsolved problems, fears, or phobias into the case. It is not always easy to find such a friend or adviser. However, if one hopes to keep level-headed and survive the turmoil of passions and emotions, the submission of one's own convictions to at least one other objective party is often essential. This is especially necessary if there is no hope or possibility of the friendship ending in a legitimate and permanent marriage. Without the help of a good counselor, it would seem advisable for young people, celibates, and married persons to avoid a situation of deep love for a person with whom one cannot be united in marriage.

To avoid the perils present in every love relationship between unmarried men and women, we should know all we can about the psychology of agape and erotic love. If a man and a woman are naively unaware of the unconscious factors at work in their relationship, they will be ill-prepared to handle the sudden eruption of sexual desire when it occurs and may abuse the God-given gift of spousal love. Sincerity, self-discipline, and unselfishness are necessary to bring eros and agape to their proper perfection; however, without dispassionate knowledge, even the most honest and self-controlled person may find himself or herself involved in a situation from which it is extremely difficult to extricate oneself.

It seems that each of us carries within the depths of our unconscious being an image of the ideal partner we would like to be united with or marry. Whether or not we realize it, we are constantly looking for the person who will fulfill and express this ideal. Unconsciously, at least, we know our limitations as an individual and our need to develop that masculinity or femininity which is incomplete within us. Psychologically we are looking for "our other half." Whenever we meet a person who more or less resembles our idea of the perfect partner, we find ourselves unusually attracted to that person. The more immature our previous personality development has been, the more magnetized and drawn are we to the one who personifies these unfulfilled needs. The more unbalanced and one-sided we are, the less control we will have over these attractions and the more easily will we be enslaved by a person who possesses what we lack in our personality.

C. G. Jung has given the name *anima* and *animus* to the two polarities of femininity and masculinity within the unconscious depths of our being. A mature man or woman will have developed to the fullest possible extent both the anima and animus so that he or she has an integrated personality, capable of handling any possible situation. At the beginning of life and, indeed, throughout most of our life, we can expect one of these polarities to be under-developed, while the opposite is over-developed. Friendships with persons of the opposite sex, if they are properly handled, are among the best means to develop a proper balance between the anima and animus within our personality. This balance between the feminine and masculine must be present in both our conscious actions and in the unconscious reactions of our psyche. Those who do not have a mature development of their anima or animus will find a strong attraction to anyone who expresses outwardly what is lacking inwardly in their own character. For example, a man who has failed to develop the gentle and tender side of his personality will be unusually attracted to a woman who exemplifies the tenderness which is missing in him. Likewise, a woman who is lacking in the security, strength, and the self-confidence commonly attributed to the mature male will find herself captivated by a man who exemplifies those qualities needed for her

151

balanced personality. On the other hand, an effeminate man will be attracted to a strong, masculine-type woman; and the choleric woman will often fall in love with a man who is gentle and easily led. In these instances the undeveloped femininity of the male and the undeveloped masculinity of the female are projected to the other person of the man-woman relationship and greatly influence it. Whenever such projection occurs, the person who carries the projection is either over-valued or under-valued.

Love can be blind to the full reality of the person to whom one is strongly attracted. However, love is also keenly perceptive of the vast potential for good present in the beloved—a potential of which that other person may still be unaware. A grave mistake is often made when it is imagined that this potential is already fully actualized in the other person. What is seen is a latent capacity which may require many years of hard work before it becomes an actuality. If everyone preparing for marriage could realize that what attracts them in the other is the aurora of possibilities of which that person is capable, a great deal of later disappointment could be avoided. This potential may be actualized at some future time.

Jungian psychologists have identified four different types of masculinity and four types of femininity. The more mature a man or woman has become, the more capable he or she is of expressing each of these four types of personality according to the need of the moment.

The four types of men are: father, eternal boy, hero (conqueror), and wise man. The four types of women are: mother, eternal girl, amazon (career woman), medium (psychic). In a mature relationship of love between man and woman each partner needs and expects to find in the other a mature expression of all four aspects of femininity or masculinity. They are all necessary if each person is to develop his/her own anima/animus. Here then are the challenges to any successful marriage or relationship of love between a man and a woman: to keep a proper tension and balance between all four facets of our sexuality and to keep a proper balance in each one of these aspects. There is both a mature and immature way to act as father, mother, eternal boy or girl, hero or amazon, wise man or medium. For example when the father image is carried to extreme, the man becomes an unbearable tyrant in the home; when the mother image is carried to the extreme, the woman becomes extremely possessive and demanding. The eternal boy carried to the extreme becomes the everlasting playboy; the eternal girl remains a flirt all her life. The hero becomes a power-hungry dictator like Hitler or Idi Amin; the amazon becomes a hard-hearted business executive. The wise man becomes someone who thinks he knows it all; the medium uses her psychic gifts for purely personal gain.

Furthermore, the discoveries of psychiatrists concerning temperaments are of invaluable assistance when men and women are making choices concerning their partner in marriage. So often a husband or wife will complain sometime after the marriage that the person they married is "not the person they were before" marriage. Either of two psychological tests, the Myers-Briggs Type Indicator or the Kiersey-Bates Temperament Sorter, (See the bibliography) if taken by both partners before marriage, or for that matter after marriage, can help one to know and understand one's dominant attitude (i.e., extravert, introvert) and dominant functions (i.e., thinking, feeling, intuition, sensation). So true is this that it is highly recommended that no man or woman should enter marriage without checking out their own temperament and that of their proposed spouse to see if there are enough points of agreement in personality to insure the success of the marriage. In most instances marriages of couples who are completely opposite in temperament end in divorce or at least result in misery until the couple can understand, admire, and respect the qualities dominant in the other. The greater the difference of temperament the more heroic and unselfish each partner must be to make a success of the marriage. But neither is it best for both spouses to be exactly the same temperament. This can make for a very dull and boring partnership that will contain no surprises and no mysteries. The more opposite are the personalities, the more love and compromises will be needed to make a happy marriage. To forbid this or that temperament to marry the opposite temperament is not the point but rather it is to give each prospective spouse a better realization of the problems and requirements involved in making a success of the marriage.

Many tragedies and broken marriages could be avoided if everyone were fully aware of the human tendency to project unconsciously our unfulfilled needs upon another. When a person is morbidly afraid of one's sexuality, there is a tendency to repress the conscious manifestations of sexual attraction. This repression usually leads to a lopsided development of personality because one projects this unexpressed side of personality upon some other person. Similarly, when people lack a proper balance of masculinity and femininity within themselves, they try to compensate by wanton behavior, imagining that they will thereby achieve the polarity which does not now exist within them. This is one reason for the unusually strong and uncontrollable desires for sexual contact that so many people in our present generation have.

To reach the proper balance and prepare ourselves for good relationships with others, we must activate our unconscious femininity or masculinity and bring it into a proper tension with our conscious feelings. There are many ways to accomplish this: for example, all that has been said in previous chapters about authenticity, shedding of masks, and educating the shadow should be considered. The reading of good fiction, participating directly or indirectly in good drama, listening to good classical music also release into our consciousness a knowledge of the inter-play of the anima and animus. However, no vicarious knowledge received from music, drama, or literature can ever completely substitute for the actual experience of personal encounters with living people.

The first experience of love is especially important. One's eyes are suddenly opened to many new values in the world. Everything is seen in a new light—the eyes of the beloved. All values in life take on a new intensity which one never believed could exist. One heard others talking about how wonderful love was, but it seemed to be so exaggerated, that is, until the experience is realized by oneself. Now one knows that love is really greater than any possible description of it. Love partakes of the infinity of God himself; and its description is beyond words or even imagination. All the books, poems, and songs about love reflect a meaning never felt in the past. Life is suddenly full of meaning.

As wonderful as this experience might be, it is important that those involved in it should realize that every encounter of love passes through three stages: spring, summer, and fall. The seeds of death are present in every human love affair, even the most intense and perfect. Even when this encounter of love results in marriage, sexual attraction and erotic love will sooner or later fade or diminish, not once but again and again. However, if both persons are willing to put forth sufficient effort and practice enough self-discipline, it is possible to experience love at a new, higher, and more spiritual level.

Happiness and fulfillment are never given ready-made to a man and woman at the beginning of their relationship of love or on the day of their marriage. This is a goal which can be expected only later in life after years of working and sacrificing together. If both are willing to rise above their selfish desires and work constantly to perfect the other, the spousal love will indeed become a satisfying marriage or friendship. Each must constantly and sincerely say to the other: "I want you to be the most perfect, happy, and fulfilled person you are capable of becoming. I will do all in my power to see that you attain the goal of your deepest and highest desires and needs. I dedicate my life to helping you fulfill all that God's providence has destined for you."

155

The mystery of Christ's death and resurrection is a principle which applies to all of life and especially to any relationship of human love. Only through the willingness to pay the price of a continual death of selfish, egotistical desires can there be achieved the rebirth and resurrection of natural, sexual love to a more spiritual, perfect love.

The sexual instinct must not be killed but often it must be sublimated into some form of unselfish love. The magnetism between the two sexes is a God-created dynamo which generates the physical and psychic energy that keeps alive all other forms of love and Christian charity between men and women. With self-control and the help of God, one can love without offending God or neighbor. Much pain may be involved in the required denial; but, at the same time, great advances in one's ability to love will also result.

It is normal to feel an attraction for a person of the opposite sex who in some way complements and completes one's self. If the energy of sex is totally obstructed, it is like trying to plug up an underground stream of tremendous psychic energy. When this stream of energy is repressed, it starts to undermine one's whole psychic being until one becomes like a swamp-land, with water oozing out of every pore. By refusing to acknowledge our desires, we force them to retreat into our unconscious underground where their psychic energy makes a marsh-land of our spiritual life, filling us with neuroses, anxieties, phobias, and other unmanageable complexes.

It is, therefore, essential that an outlet for these energies be found in some form of legitimate friendship, endeavoring always to live in accord with justice and truth as indicated by our intellect, good judgment, common sense, and the best interests of everyone concerned or involved. If one trusts solely the physical attraction, one will soon find that these desires drown out the intellectual and other spiritual powers of one's being. As a result, one soon will become enslaved to sex and the all-consuming desire for sexual pleasure. By self-discipline we must learn to redirect these energies into a more agapistic love for the community as a whole.

It is possible, but extremely difficult, to lead a full life on earth without ever participating in the physical sex act. However, it is never possible to develop one's personality or to carry out our functions of love for God and neighbor if we sacrifice completely our eros, i.e., the spiritual, psychic love for the counterpart of our anima and animus. This deep-seated erotic love in every human being must be brought into balance with the rest of our personality and put to good use through lawful encounters of friendship with persons of the other sex; otherwise it will undermine and destroy the effectiveness of much of our life on earth.

It is strongly recommended that in any encounter of love everything be done to delay the manifestations of sexual desire as long as possible. This is appropriate in order to make room for the possible union of spirit before the physical union. If physical attraction develops and is expressed more quickly than spiritual love, it will often be impossible to have a true friendship with the person to whom one feels so strongly drawn. Physical attraction can be felt toward many persons; the total commitment of spousal love should be given to only one person. Polygamy and polyandry are practices which are found in cultures or civilizations still undeveloped and immature. Anyone who has experienced the fullness of spousal love will realize that it could not possibly be shared at the same time with more than one person.

On the other hand, it is possible to have a mature friendship with many persons of the opposite sex. Erotic love will be present in some way in each of these friendships; but with proper restraint it can be kept within control. These friendships may well be the impetus to vitalize our whole life and all our relationships with others; whereas, the absence of such friendships will often result in a loss of flexibility, enthusiasm, and a decrease in the energy to live. Even our prayer life benefits from any bonafide human encounter of love with a person of the opposite sex. Therefore, despite the dangers present in friendships between men and women, the advantages of these encounters outweigh the disadvantages. If the love can be fulfilled in a permanent and publicly recognized marriage, the problems of love do not disappear but usually can be handled more capably.

But what about the situations where marriage is not possible or feasible? Consider the husbands and wives who find themselves in an impossible situation where the other partner refuses to make a return of love, or where because of incompatibility or other valid reasons, no encounter of spousal love is possible between them? What about celibates—priests, nuns, and others—who feel called or compelled to adopt a life of total abstinence from connubial pleasure? These are some of the situations of life which are extremely difficult. Each one must be considered individually; and by prayer, grace, intelligence, intuition, and the experience of others, the proper wisdom to resolve each situation will be discovered. The resolution of some cases seems absolutely impossible at first sight; but with patience and sacrifice, God's will can be discovered and fulfilled.

To find the right solution, previous commitments, obligations and responsibilities should be honored as far as possible. There must be a proper regard for laws, customs, danger of scandal, and any evils that might result from a particular decision. A proper order must be established so that the greatest amount of good is done for the most people and the least amount of harm to the fewest persons. There is seldom a black and white case with all the good on one side and all the harm on the other. In each situation the rights and needs of others must be considered; otherwise, there could be no true, lasting encounter of love and no full enjoyment of friendship by the persons involved. Sometimes one must be heroic enough to sacrifice the possibility of ever enjoying a shared love on earth with this or that particular person because great harm would accrue to others from the continuation of a particular friendship.

To find the heroism and courage to make the right decisions, it is necessary to have a deep faith and love of God along with a strong belief in the existence of an eternal life after death where ultimate justice will be rendered and the satisfaction of our basic needs and desires for love is finally attained. To reach perfect love is impossible on earth; but since all earthly life is a preparation for a more perfect life after death, we must find the strength to sacrifice earthly joys, when necessary, for a heavenly life where true love and friendship with God and mankind will exist forever.

All that has been written in this chapter concerns persons who are heterosexual. What can be said about those many people in today's society who are homosexual? It would seem that everyone should attempt to make conscious whatever heterosexuality is present in one's unconscious psyche, at the same time realistically recognizing any homosexuality, either conscious or unconscious. The same guidelines recommended above for heterosexual relationships apply also to homosexual friendships: namely, the necessary safeguards to prevent more harm than good from occurring. Those interested should consult the literature of *Dignity*, a religious organization dedicated to helping homosexually inclined men and women discover how best to fulfill God's will in this situation.

CHAPTER SEVENTEEN

NO MAN IS AN ISLAND

No one can struggle with the tasks of love and maturity without realizing before long how much we depend upon others and they upon us. In every area of life, we see the need of community and of help from each other. For continued growth in character and personality we must constantly give and receive love and aid. The more giving and receiving there is between us, the more quickly we will grow to the wholeness for which we as individuals have been destined and the sooner all mankind will attain that goal of unity willed for it by our Creator.

Every act of unselfish giving accomplishes many worthwhile and needed tasks on earth: it pleases God, fulfills the purpose of our existence, gives us a sense of well-being and fulfillment, makes others feel worthwhile and loveable, helps others overcome feelings of inferiority and insecurity, hastens the great day of the Lord when Christ will establish his visible kingdom of love "where God will be all in all" (I Cor. 15:28).

However, living in community with our brethren can be both a hindrance and a help to our growth in wholeness. There are times when we need to withdraw from our fellow men and face ourselves alone in the presence of God. We need vacations even from those whom we love most dearly and who also love us. In a certain sense we need vacations from God, from prayers, and from the practice of our religious duties. During these moments alone, we must not do anything to hurt or displease God or our beloved friends; but for our inner growth and for the hope of being able afterwards to give the greatest possible service to God and our human brethren, we need periods of quiet and peace to recharge our spiritual batteries so that we can return to the community with renewed strength and vigor to fulfill our tasks.

Sometimes community life can hang like a yoke around our necks, perhaps because we dislike being one among so many and we imagine that the presence of others hinders our development as individuals. On the other hand, to reach maturity without the presence and aid of the community is impossible; we cannot fulfill the purpose of our existence unless there are other persons to be loved and to love us. At times some vital experience of the solidarity of the human race can bring forcibly home how much we do need one another. These experiences of our creatureliness help us to overcome the pride and selfishness whereby we seek an independence that belongs properly only to God.

The realization of the universal brotherhood of mankind and the need of community is an essential trait of the mature person. Maturity and authenticity are based upon truth, and it is a simple fact that we all are creatures dependent upon God Almighty. To fulfill our obligations of love toward our brethren, we need to be unmistakably aware of the vast distance which separates the Creator from his creatures. At first, we resist the humiliation connected with the knowledge of our creatureliness; but, as it grows on us, a wonderful feeling of understanding, fellowship, and oneness with the other members of the human race results. We are glad to be a part of mankind, to cooperate in helping others attain their individual destinies, and to work with them for common goals and the universal good.

Any situation of "need and help" will contribute to the recognition of our dependence and appreciation of the value of community. If we happen to be the one who needs the help of others, or if we see someone who needs our help, the result will be the same. The more serious the need of help, the more quickly our feeling of solidarity will evolve. For example, suppose we see a total stranger in danger of drowning. Forgetting the risk to our life, we plunge into the water and extend a hand to the man who so desperately needs our help. When the crisis is over, both the saved and the savior come to appreciate the value and need of each other. In that moment of common danger we will have learned the fact of our dependence upon one another.

Another situation that helps us to appreciate our common brotherhood is the experience of guilt that follows some sin or fault which has hurt another member of the community. For example, suppose through our negligence and carelessness we strike a child with our car and kill him. We have inflicted irreparable damage upon another and are filled with shame and even despair at the realization of our inability to remedy our mistake. A real danger here is a total collapse of our inner being and a complete loss of faith and trust in ourselves. However, instead of losing faith, we may find ourselves gradually filled with a deep sense of compassion and empathy for all other human beings who have suffered a similar guilt. We begin to understand that all of us need redemption (rescuing) and salvation (reprieve). We no longer feel alone in our guilt or isolated from the rest of the community; instead, we feel that we are very much a part of ordinary mankind. No longer can we look down upon others from an attitude of false superiority. We have been introduced to one of the basic truths of mankind: we are all brothers of one flesh and blood, prone to the same deficiencies. We have made contact through our sufferings with the common foundation of all human beings: our creatureliness. We are now ready to join the universal brotherhood of man and work for the betterment of all. "What can we do together to bring everyone to the goals of love and maturity for which we have been destined by our

Creator?" In some mysterious way the solidarity of the human race makes all of us dependent upon one another.

As far as possible we must identify ourselves with our brethren and with each individual in the community. We must try to put ourselves into their "skin", as Atticus tells us in Harper Lee's novel, "To Kill a Mockingbird," and to see the world through their eyes and understand why they speak or act as they do. If we are successful, we will find a beautiful empathy developing within our heart toward every brother and sister who is suffering or in need. Without waiting until we are asked, our hearts will go out to them and see their needs, even before they themselves become aware of him. This is the kind of brotherly love upon which every friendship and every community must be based.

The stronger personalities of the community have the greatest obligation to show love and empathy to those in need. Most people are willing to follow a strong leader. Therefore, whenever a strong personality succeeds in triumphing over sin, selfishness, and other faults, the rest of the community finds it considerably easier to rise above their own selfishness and weaknesses.

If the stronger individual fails to come to the aid of his weaker sister or brother, a complete collapse in the suffering party may result. In every community some individuals are unable to bear the burdens of life alone. Our mental hospitals are filled with these weak souls who could have been saved from the living death they now suffer, if someone had been thoughtful enough to reach out to them in love at some earlier period in their lives. We might ask ourselves, "What would have been our lot in life, if we had not received the love of which others have given us so generously?" If we have had the good fortune to have received unselfish love from parents and others, we are more capable of forgetting our selfish wants and occupying ourselves in loving service to others. Those who have never experienced unselfish love need the encouragement and confidence which come from being loved so that they too can find the courage to go out to others in loving service.

The talents and strength we now have do not really belong to us alone. They are the gifts of God and of the family and the community in which we have been placed. They should be used to help others rather than kept for our pleasure and benefit. Our final perfection depends upon how unselfishly we share our material, physical, psychological, and spiritual wealth with others. Even though our present talents and ability to love might be exceedingly limited, we must not sit idly by and wait until further help and love is bestowed on us; let us make use of every opportunity we have and give ourselves in loving service to others.

Even the strongest personalities in the community need our love, especially in times of great strain and crisis. Regardless of how brave and strong a person seems to be, "no man is an island." In his mercy and wisdom God has left all of us with an Achilles heel: namely, those limitations of personality where we stand most in need of others. This mutual dependence upon one another is the means God uses to bring us closer together so that all people will become united in his kingdom of love. Without friends and friendships, life on earth would be unbearable. Just as Jesus needed the strength given him by his Blessed Mother and his other friends standing beneath the cross, so we need others and others need us whenever there is sickness, death, or trouble of any kind. It is not always necessary that we offer external help; our very presence often gives others the strength to bear their cross. The heroic acts of love and suffering endured by Christ have helped countless millions of Christians to love and to carry their cross.

Sometimes our overtures of love are rebuffed. If so, it is usually because of fear, ignorance, or bad experiences of rejection in the past. We should not become discouraged but try harder to convince others of the sincerity of our love and willingness to help. It may take repeated efforts to break through their fears and skepticism. Perhaps the time may not be ripe for us to prove our love, but we should not desist. Using whatever experience, common sense, and wisdom we possess, we should be ready and willing to love and serve others whenever the opportunity presents itself.

If we open our hearts humbly and beseechingly, others will usually accept our love and friendship. People reject paternalism and the humiliation which comes from the condescension a proud person shows in his manner of giving. Any pride and superiority we feel will be resented and prevent us from helping them. We are willing to be helped openly by a fellow brother or sister.

It is amazing what others can do once we have convinced them of our sincere love and belief in them. Previously they may have been paralyzed by fear, insecurity, an inferiority complex, or other inhibitions. When they finally find someone who believes in them and their worth, they suddenly come to life, discovering within themselves powers, energies, and abilities never previously suspected. They begin to develop the reserves of spiritual and physical energy which lie buried in the depths of every human being. The faith which we show in them is the spark that starts this whole process of uncovering, discovering, and developing their potential for loving service to the community. Without the stimulus of our love and confidence, they might very well have lived and died without anyone, least of all themselves, suspecting that they were capable of so much power to love and to do good for God, their brethren, and the world.

However, to stop thinking constantly about ourselves and what people think of us requires some courage and effort on our part. By taking a real interest in others and trying to discover their many hidden talents, we find there is a real potential of goodness present in every human being. Instead of imagining the world and others to be so terrible and full of sin, we must find the faith to believe in the possibilities for good in everyone. The extremes to which we are willing to go to help them will show clearly the degree of our sincerity in the protestations of faith and love we have made to them. Even with our sincerest and best efforts, we can expect some failures in our attempts to extend ourselves in love; but as long as we keep trying to reach out to others with a heart full of love, the good results of our endeavors will outweigh whatever strain or suffering befalls us.

As we grow in love for the community of our fellow human beings, our self-sufficiency as an individual should diminish. Like a piece of rubber, we will feel ourselves pulled in every direction by the demands of those around us. We will begin to feel like a man stretched upon a cross, and our whole ego will seem to be dying. We then will experience our own great need of help, and we will open our heart even wider to receive assistance from God and from anyone who is willing to come to our aid. We begin to realize how inadequate we are, when alone, to take care of the many things that need to be done for the community. If we have truly conquered our selfishness and have kept ourselves receptive to God and to others, then at the very moment when we feel ourselves stretched to the utmost of our capacity, we will discover that we have made a new contact with immense inner powers totally beyond our conscious faculties and strength. We are tapping the powers of our unconscious self. Beyond these unconscious energies, we also make contact with the infinite powers of God. We feel ourselves permeated by God's own life of love. As a result, we receive from God the needed healing powers for ourselves which will extend from us to the community.

In this moment of greatest openness our whole body takes on a transparency which enables our soul to shine forth in much the same way as the apostles saw Christ's body on the mountain at the transfiguration. Our eyes become windows which allow the inner light of our being to be seen by others. Our face and skin become radiant like the face of Moses when he came down from his encounter with God on Mount Sinai. Every gesture and facial expression beautifully expresses our desire to go out of ourselves and give ourselves entirely in love for others.

166

CHAPTER EIGHTEEN

LOVING OUR ENEMIES

"You have heard that it was said of old, 'You shall love your neighbor and hate your enemy,' but I tell you, love your enemies, do good to those who hate you and pray for those who persecute and calumniate you, that you may be sons of your Father in heaven. For he makes his sun rise upon evil men as well as good, and he sends his rain upon honest and dishonest men alike. If you love only those who love you, what credit is that to you? And if you exchange greetings with your own circle, are you doing anything exceptional? Even the pagans do that much. No, you are to be perfect as your Heavenly Father" (Matt. 5:43-48).

One of the tests for true maturity is the ability to love our enemies as Christ loved his enemies. But, before we can love them, we must first recognize the two classes of enemies who threaten us: (1) the inner enemies present in the depth of our soul; (2) the human enemies among our brethren. Both of these enemies must be loved in a special way; yet there is an interdependence of our love for these enemies.

Our Inner Enemies

To recognize and love our inner enemies is most important of all; otherwise, we will never love properly our external enemies. As we have seen in Chapter Eight, much of the evil we imagine, or actually see, in others is the projection of our own repressed faults. The inner feelings of guilt resulting from this repression build up a pressure and an indefinable anxiety which is temporarily relieved by a projection upon another—a fellow human being, Satan, or even God. As soon as we uncover and admit these repressed evil tendencies within us, our hostilities toward our outer enemies usually subside. Therefore, most of the problems of hostility must be solved primarily within the inner world of our conscious and unconscious life. The better we understand ourselves and our repressed shadow, the more easily we will be able to love our external enemies.

Besides the unconscious shadow which is scorned and rejected, there is in many people a very real and deep hatred for themselves. Because they fail to measure up to some false standard chosen through pride or wrong education, they lose respect for their real worth. Unable to achieve this false ideal, they come to abhor their weaknesses and creatureliness. Instead of loving themselves as God commands them to do, they hate themselves.

At least half the battle in conquering our inner enemies is to uncover, recognize, and accept personal ownership of them. Then we must see their worth and learn to love them and put them to good use. If we fail to find adequate expression for these inner drives, the result will be a schizoid or split personality. We must openly acknowledge to ourselves the presence of these evil tendencies and admit them to at least one other human being whose judgment we trust and who agrees with us that we do, indeed, have within us the enemies we suspected.

Once we have acknowledged their presence, we must find a way to change the direction of the energies behind each of these inclinations. Not everything about them is bad; they are evil because they have gone astray in pursuit of a false goal. They are like wayward children who must be given extra care in their correction and training. Rather than disown, despise, or hate these weaknesses, we must understand them and search for a way to put them to good use to help our growth of character and to aid others around us. If we succeed in handling properly these inner enemies, we will have found also the key to loving and handling our outer enemies. The answer lies in accepting each day the cross of self-denial and following Christ in the total commitment or our will to the will of the Heavenly Father. The energy, which we use to please ourselves and to exalt our own ego-image before others, must be redirected toward God, the welfare of our neighbor, and the integration of our whole personality with all that is good.

Traditionally, the Church has summed up these inner enemies in the seven Capital sins: pride, sloth, envy, anger, lust, gluttony, and covetousness (avarice). To this list might be added vanity, selfishness, dishonesty, fear, and any particular fault of which we are aware. One by one these transgressions, which we are too often ashamed to admit to ourselves, must be exposed and converted into good. Behind every fault there is a potential virtue. If we can only succeed in changing the direction of this psychic energy now being wasted on some useless or evil pursuit, we will soon discover that these inner enemies are enemies no longer.

Pride is setting up our ego as king and worshipping our inner self as a false god. When guilty of pride, we have fallen head over heels in love with ourselves and have made ourselves, rather than God, the center of the universe. If we can succeed in falling in love with God, we will be able to direct toward God all the energy previously dissipated on ourselves. By a denial of our egotism, the energy of pride is put to work making God the king and center of the universe and our inner self merely the center of our own personality. In the Gospels we find that Jesus Christ never tried to kill the ambition of his apostles but sought only to give their energy a proper direction. "If any man wishes to be first, he shall be the last of all and the servant of all" (Mk. 9:35). "Whoever humbles himself as this little child, he is the greatest in the kingdom of heaven" (Matt. 18:4).

At first sight, sloth seems to be a lack of energy; but it is rather the directing of our efforts toward the avoidance of work, pain, and self-denial of any kind. Behind this attempt to escape from labor and suffering, there is an appreciation of the need of leisure, relaxation, and quiet. A person with an "energy neurosis" is just as unbalanced as the one who is always procrastinating. As the author of Ecclesiastes says, "There is a season for everything, a time for every occupation under heaven" (Eccl. 3:1). Our Lord's praise of Mary, the sister of Martha, is proof enough that we need periods of quiet every day to contemplate the things of God and appreciate the spiritual value. Our activity will be more productive of good when it is the result and overflow of quiet, prayer, and meditation.

Envy is a misdirection of the energies of competition which God has placed in every healthy, normal human being. Rather than resent others who possess something we lack, our efforts should be directed to the utmost fulfillment of our own potential. The real contest is within ourselves, not with other persons. There would be no real problem with envy if all our competitive energies were directed to conquering our own mediocrity and attaining the high ideals God has implanted in our nature. "All the runners at the stadium are trying to win, but only one of them gets the prize. You must run in the same way, meaning to win" (I Cor. 9:24).

Anger is the desire to attack violently anyone or anything which we consider a threat to our well-being or to the well-being of someone or something we cherish. The powerful energies of anger can accomplish much good if

170

they are used in a proportionate degree against a real enemy who endangers our welfare or the welfare of someone we love. If the forces behind anger are properly directed, we will become totally dedicated to the pursuit of justice for the down-trodden, the poor, and the helpless. In the Gospels we see the anger of Christ used very effectively to obtain the proper respect for the Heavenly Father, for God's temple, and for the protection of the poor and helpless sinners. "Let her alone; why must you make her feel uncomfortable? She has done a beautiful thing for me" (Mk. 14:6).

Lust, gluttony, and avarice have the same basic nature; the unrestrained and selfish desire for power and pleasure. Lust for forbidden sexual pleasure is the energy of love which has been misdirected. Instead of allowing an unlawful sexual desire to be dissipated in one's own pleasure, it must be sublimated into a legitimate desire to serve others and help them reach the fulfillment of God's purpose in their regard. Gluttony, like lust, can be redirected and converted into a spiritual hunger and thirst for justice, love and all the worthwhile values in life. Avarice, the other member of this trio, can become an intense desire to share with the needy all our wealth. The striving for material wealth and other forms of worldly goods can be transformed by the dedication of our energies to a more equal distribution of the good things of this earth. No longer is it a selfish covetousness but a struggle to apportion both material and spiritual goods among all mankind.

A vain and exaggerated desire for beauty can be more properly directed to a keen appreciation of all the beautiful things of heaven and earth. Our love for beauty is not wrong as long as it is balanced with a love for truth and goodness. Even self-love is not evil when we give it and other recipients of our love the right order in our life. In the second great commandment of both the Old and New Testament we are told to love our neighbor as we love ourselves. The evil of selfishness is present when we love ourselves to the exclusion of God and neighbor.

171

A great deal of energy is expended in fleeing from the truth. Dishonesty is a misdirection of the desire to protect our integrity and security. God expects us to avoid anything which would destroy us or shatter our equilibrium provided it can be done without doing even greater harm to someone. If we have been properly instructed, we will realize that there can be no security for us unless we stand solidly in the truth. Therefore, all our efforts for the well-being of ourselves and others will accomplish the greatest good if we have an overwhelming love and desire for the truth, regardless of the cost. There is no valid goodness or security in the world unless it is grounded on truth.

Perhaps the most dangerous of all our inner enemies is fear. A neurotic and unreasonable fear is the result of an exaggerated idea of what is expected of us and a lack of proper appreciation of God's goodness, power, wisdom, and love. It is not wrong to have a healthy respect for God's power and a desire for the respect of others. If one has sufficient humility, faith, and confidence in God, the energies dissipated on fear can become a zeal and enthusiasm for good. If we have a firm faith in God's mercy, wisdom, power, and love, we will not be afraid. Trusting ourselves completely to God's loving providence, we will use in a constructive way the energies formerly wasted on fear.

Our Outer Enemies

If we succeed in correcting our false ideals and find the right goals for our lives, many of our supposed outer enemies will be seen as friends and benefactors. One of the greatest benefits reaped from external enemies is that they help us to recognize our secret, unconscious faults. Frequently others are clever enough to hit upon our Achilles heel and reveal to us something we should know about ourselves but never would have discovered without their help. Without judging the goodness or baseness of our persecutor's intentions, we can always be grateful to anyone who helps us to know the full truth about ourselves.

To learn to love our outer enemies is often an exceedingly slow and laborious task; but it is a satisfaction to know that it is one of the last and highest tasks in our growth toward wholeness. There must be no hypocrisy or pretense in the love we feel for those who hurt us. If we feel hatred and anger, it is better to admit to ourselves these resentments; otherwise, we continue to repress our feelings, and the animosity we feel toward others is driven even deeper into our unconscious psyche. Perhaps, after a number of experiences with our persecutors, we will realize they can't really harm us but only help us. If we remember that God can bring good out of everything, we will no longer be afraid of others. They may make us suffer, but they will not increase our inner darkness. The anguish we feel from their persecutions can be a growing pain which takes us another step toward our goal.

It is not always possible to make peace with our adversaries; even Christ was unable to do this. However, we should not be too quick to place the blame on the other person. If we are truly unselfish, our efforts at peacemaking will often be irresistible. Before we arrive at this perfection, we can at least use the enmity of others to discover our shadow, admit it, convert it, change its direction, and assimilate its energy into the pursuit of good. When we have succeeded in purifying and redeeming our unconscious evil, we will find that our fears of external enemies will turn into gratitude and our hatred into love.

"You have heard that it used to be said, 'An eye for an eye and a tooth for a tooth,' but I tell you, don't resist the evil doers. If a man hits you on the right cheek, turn to him the other also. If a man wants to take away your coat, let him have your cloak as well. If someone forces you to go a mile, go two miles with him" (Matt. 5:38-41). This Christian philosophy of non-resistance to evil is not easy to practice, especially if we are selfish and fearful. The advice of Christ is not meant for public institutions, such as the city, state, or nation. We are not to do away with the police force or allow bullies to exploit their victims. Christ's instruction is to help the individual Christian control the instinct of self-preservation and prevent it from being dominated by egocentricity. Christ says that, if our dignity is rooted in an honest relationship with God and we are aware of our inner strength, a slap in the face will not devastate us or inflict any serious harm upon us. Whatever reaction we have to evil that others heap upon us should be determined by a sincere judgment of what will do the most good for everyone concerned, including our persecutors.

Non-resistance to the evil-doer must be sincere, neither pretended nor resulting from a cowardly fear of the oppressor. Instead of returning evil for evil we should relax and let the attack sweep over us. The first few experiences will be the most difficult and will be endured purely on blind faith in the value of Christ's words. Gradually, if we are properly humble, the practice of non-resistance to evil will redound immensely to our benefit. The suffering imposed on us by the evil-doer awakens the creative powers of our unconscious being until we become capable of bringing good out of evil. We become conscious of our hidden faults which, otherwise, would have remained unknown to us. We gain inner strength and peace as the acceptance of suffering helps us to stand more and more securely in God's truth. We identify ourselves more easily with Jesus Christ in his passion and death.

Sometimes, our patient endurance of evil brings about the conversion of the evil-doer. At other times, the other person becomes even more harsh in his persecution, since our non-resistance makes his own evil all the more self-evident. Regardless of the effect on the other person, our refusal to return evil for evil at least prevents any addition to the iniquities already in existence.

If we are to obey Christ's command to pray sincerely for our enemies, we must try to see the whole situation from God's point of view. What good can God bring out of this suffering for me, for the persecutor, and for others? We must allow the sunshine of our love and the gentle rain of our prayers to fall upon our enemies and transform whatever is cold, mean, or ugly in them into the warm, living embrace of love. Instead of allowing ourselves to indulge in hateful and destructive thoughts which will only add to the evil already in existence, we must return a blessing for a curse, contributing something positive and good for every negative element in the other's actions or words.

Hostility to God

To accuse one of hating God may seem an exaggeration to most decent people. Nevertheless, there is present within the unconscious depths of all of us a certain hostility to God. We sometimes see him as the one who stands between us and the pursuit of our happiness and best interests. We cannot commit a deliberate sin, mortal or venial, unless we, first of all, feel a certain hatred of God. Before we can deliberately disobey any of God's commands, we must persuade ourselves that God's plan for us is not for our good and that we know better than God what is best for us.

A frequent cause of hostility toward God is the false, distorted image of God which we have adopted. This is usually due to a faulty religious education in youth when God has been presented as an ogre ready to condemn and punish us for the slightest miscue on our part. In this situation it is not the real God that we are hating or rejecting but the wrong picture of God.

However, there is also a very legitimate hostility we can feel toward certain aspects of the true God, which are indeed very mysterious and terrifying. Besides the fascinating, lovable side of God, there is also an awesome, stern, and serious side in the divine personality. Both the Old and New Testaments of the Bible give us these opposing poles of the person of God. In contrast to the loving mother and father image of God given by Second Isaiah (Chapter 49) and Hosea (Chapter 11), we are also

175

presented with a God that destroys and wreaks vengeance on anyone who opposes him. Similarly, in the Gospels, Jesus speaks not only of a divine shepherd who goes in search of a lost sheep but also of an eternal fire where the worms do not die and the fire is not extinguished (Mark 9:48).

The real core of most of our hostility to God lies in the fact that God stands between us and an unlimited exercise of our freedom. We dislike using our power of freedom in moderation or according to the limitations God has laid down for its use. Finding our independence so delightful, we want to be complete masters of our lives without anyone or anything to hinder us. We consider every denial of pleasure which God asks of us as an intrusion upon our precious freedom and, consequently, use it as an excuse for showing resentment and hostility to our Creator. Frequently we rationalize our sin or temptation by blaming it upon Satan or some external enemy. That others often share in the responsibility for our sin cannot be denied; but ultimately the cause of sin is found within our own wayward heart. To relieve this burden of guilt we often try to project our evil and anger upon God or someone other than ourselves.

CHAPTER NINETEEN

ENCOUNTERS WITH GOD

Since religion is primarily a loving encounter between God's person and our person, there is a most intimate connection between our capacity for natural, human love and our capacity for encounter with God. By grace, the person of God touches our inner self and fills us with God's own life of love. Unless we have developed the natural powers for love within our soul, it is often impossible to enter to a full, loving union with God. God can work a miracle of grace and substitute directly for any deficiency of human love in our life. We can hope for this to happen if, through no fault of our own, we have been deprived of good experiences of natural love. However, it is our responsibility to do everything possible to foster the growth of natural love in our lives so that we can encounter God to the utmost limits of our potential.

Natural love loosens the soil of the soul making it soft and pliable to the actions of God's grace. Each personal encounter of human love is a preparation for that religious surrender of our life to God which we call faith. Our natural experiences of love activate the energies of enthusiasm within us and give us the vitality needed for the heroic practice of our Christian faith. If love is an active force within our life, our whole being will become radiant with physical, mental, and emotional energy and health. Our bodies will be transparent and glowing with the desire to go out to others and give ourselves in love to mankind and God.

Both love and religion have the same mortal enemy: selfishness; and they have the same goal: the redemption of our whole being from the isolation of self. Every encounter of love increases our power to love at other levels. Every good friendship profoundly influences our whole life for the better. On the other hand, natural, human love cannot continue indefinitely upon earth without some contact with God and religion. Without the benefits that love and religion can give each other, there is a tendency for both our spiritual and human encounters to degenerate into a union of things on a neutral level instead of a real unity of persons.

Without a living, growing contact between our person and the person of God, we will not achieve or maintain any substantial degree of maturity in our personality. During the first half of life we do not feel the need of God as desperately as after the age of thirty-five or forty. In early adulthood we are often so occupied with carving a niche for ourselves here on earth that religious duties are postponed or neglected. However, around the age of forty almost everyone begins to realize that in this short life span it will never be possible to fulfill all one's ambitions and desires. Without a strong faith in God and the practice of religion at this time, most persons will experience one or another neurotic symptom: psychosomatic illnesses of the body; unexplained and unjustified fears; anxieties and scruples; a general lack of inner security, self-confidence, balance, order, and harmony in the conscious areas of life. Even when stronger personalities are able to repress these stirrings of their unconscious being in its search for God, they cannot hide their restlessness, impatience, irritability, and general dissatisfaction with themselves, with those around them, and with everything on earth. Often these tribulations are projected upon others so that the non-religious person becomes excessively critical and harsh in his judgments and condemnations. Without God, even our natural life lacks warmth, sensitivity, and creativity; instead it becomes cold, depressing, and unproductive.

St. Augustine once cried out: "Our hearts were made for thee, O God, and they shall not rest until they rest in thee." In the depths of every human soul there is a desire to know and encounter God. Carl Gustav Jung was the first modern depth psychologist to discover this deepest stratum of the human unconscious and named these religious needs of the human psyche the collective, religious archetypes of man. Jung categorically states that, in his contacts with hundreds of mentally ill patients from every country in the world, never did he find a mentally or emotionally disturbed person over the age of thirty-five whose problem was not primarily religious. He further states that it was impossible for him to help these disturbed patients until he succeeded in finding some way for them to make satisfactory contact with a Supreme Being upon whom they were willing to depend. Jung felt that this lack of religion is the prime cause of much of the restlessness and imbalance in people today.

Therefore, it is quite necessary that we develop these religious archetypes and make them active, living influences in our daily activities. Without an activation of the religious needs that lie deep within our psyche, our personality will lack wholeness and balance. Through these archetypes we are able to make real encounters of love with God's person and by these religious encounters grow to the fullness of perfection for which we have been destined.

The two basic natural religious archetypes become conscious whenever we experience either the *tremendous* or the *fascinating* aspects of God's nature. The fearful tremendousness of God is seen in his mighty power, his awesome majesty, his divine justice, his infinite truth, his strict and final judgments, his destruction of those nations and persons who thwart his purposes, his eternal punishments and rewards. In contrast to the majesty which threatens to overwhelm us, we find ourselves also attracted to the many fascinating facets of God's personality: his infinite kindness, goodness, love, mercy, forgiveness; his immense beauty, order, and harmony; his promises of eternal salvation and happiness.

At first sight, these two views of God seem contradictory. We are caught between a desire to run away in fear from his overwhelming grandeur and an equally strong desire to run toward him in love and be engulfed by his infinite kindness, beauty, goodness, and love.

It is usually impossible for these natural religious archetypes to accomplish a proper balance between the two poles of God's awesome power and his equally infinite beauty, goodness, love, and gentleness. Either we become so terribly afraid of God that we seek to escape from him, his judgments, and his punishments or so familiar with him that we imagine that God will never punish us no matter what evil we might deliberately choose. In past generations many people experienced an exaggerated idea of God's majesty. They became excessively afraid of sin and hell and imagined that few people could hope to escape God's terrible vengeance. Recently, as a reaction to this extreme of fear, many people state categorically that there is no such thing as sin, hell, or punishment after death. They say, "God is too good to send anyone to hell." This is then used as an excuse for doing away with all inhibition of guilt of sin.

Our natural religious archetypes need to be elevated and converted by the grace of Christ; otherwise, we will find ourselves going to one extreme or another in our encounters with God. A study of Jesus' life will reveal to us many occasions when we see both the over-powering awesomeness and the extremely fascinating beauty and attractiveness of God. We have an example of the dilemma when Peter, after the miracle of the catch of fish, fell at the feet of Christ and begged, "Depart from me, O Lord, for I am a sinful man" (Lk. 5:8). Even though Peter said this, it was not what his heart really desired. He was caught between the overwhelming attraction of Jesus' personality and an equally strong sense of his own unworthiness.

In the beginning of our encounters with God, nature and grace often proceed peacefully hand in hand. However, as we progress in a knowledge of God and nature, we discover the separation which exists between the revelation of God found in the New Testament and a merely natural relationship with God. Natural religion loves its freedom and reacts violently against any rigid dogmas or confining laws of morality. Natural religion exaggerates the value of private, personal religious encounters and often resents joining a community in worshipping God. It considers contacts with others a hindrance rather than a help to a free, individual, religious experience. Having to join with others in participation at Mass or other liturgical service becomes a distraction rather than an aid to a person whose religious outlook on life is primarily natural. Natural religion actually makes man rather than God the center of faith and worship since its religious practices are based exclusively on our natural knowledge of God apart from divine revelation. In this way man is freed to determine his own religious rules and to please himself rather than God.

Natural religious archetypes need to be awakened; and they must be converted and liberated by contact with Christ. When an encounter with Christ is made, there will be a clash and perhaps an open declaration of war between our natural religious ideas and God's revelation as found in Sacred Scripture. Anyone who has not undergone this conflict between his natural desires and God's will as manifested and taught by Jesus Christ will seldom have a full encounter with God. This struggle between nature and grace is essential, and no one can consider himself a mature Christian until he has experienced it.

The confrontation between Christ and our natural religious ideas should begin with a comparison between the two so that we can appreciate more clearly the different goals and requirements of both. Natural religion demands only that we recognize a superior being but leaves us to determine what our obligations of God should be. Jesus Christ demands that we be willing to sacrifice everything and everyone dear to us, when necessary, to carry out the duties imposed on us by the Gospel. (Cf. the rich young man: Mark 10, Matthew 19).

In early life, our total absorption in the things of this earth often keeps us from recognizing this challenge which Christ and Christianity give. However, sooner or later, everyone must make this decision of being either entirely for or totally against Christ. Only when this dilemma is fully realized do we become capable of making a mature act of faith and experience a true commitment to Christ and God.

If the decision is against Christ, there will be an increase in one's rebellion and hostility to God. There is a real danger that, rather than humbling ourselves before the demands of the Gospel, we will settle for some man-centered, natural way of religion where the true God is removed from his exalted throne and is made an equal to us so that we can encounter him in perfect freedom and independence. To satisfy our religious instincts, we will then look for some false god with whom we can be joined in some kind of religious commitment. Sometimes it is a commitment to the pursuit of wealth or power or pleasure or some other worldly ambition. If we feel especially altruistic, our natural religion takes the form of secular humanism which makes a god out of mere humanity.

If parents, teachers, and religious leaders have faced the challenge between nature and Christ in their own lives and have solved their crisis of faith by a total commitment to Christ and the Gospels, they will be able to guide those under their tutelage to a proper confrontation with the demands of Jesus Christ. If the leader has either failed to experience this personal challenge of Jesus or has actually rejected the way of the Gospels and chosen some form of natural religion, the effect upon those with whom he has contact will usually be disastrous.

The confrontation with Jesus Christ should be made gradually and a full clash delayed until a person has developed some maturity; otherwise much harm can be expected. Even when the confrontation is delayed until adulthood, some will undoubtedly decide against Christ. This is the freedom of choice God gives each of us. But, those who decide to accept the requirements of the Gospel will experience a new and wonderful fullness of life.

To make a Christian commitment and to enter into a valid religious encounter with Christ and through Christ with the real God are not easy. God and Christ are quite different from what we might naturally expect. They are much more demanding of us than we would prefer. Therefore, to accept Jesus Christ, we must bring about a profound conversion of many of our ideas concerning God. Having undergone this *metanoia*, there must be a total submission of our judgment and will to the revelation of God, to the teachings of the Gospel, and to the authentic inspiration of the Holy Spirit.

God never compels our assent; he insists that we remain free. God does not wish to destroy nature but only to convert it so that we might experience a resurrection and elevation to a higher form of life. Our nature rebels against the remolding which is required; we cherish the things that we must often forego in order to be a whole-hearted Christian. Just as the rich young man in the Gospels was scandalized and saddened by the high price Jesus asked of him, so today many persons sadly turn away when they are asked to sacrifice something they hold near and dear to become Christ's disciples. If they would only ask someone who has made the sacrifice and become Christ's true follower, they would be told—just as Peter, James, and John could have told the rich man—that these sacrifices are a small price to pay for the unlimited spiritual riches received in return. But many of us like to be independent and completely uninhibited. We want to do as we please and believe as we choose, without any outside restrictions. The sacrifice of the desire to be a law unto ourselves is the essence of the price which must be paid to encounter the true God revealed by Jesus Christ rather than some false god which we have invented to satisfy our selfish fancy.

The scandal of the Christian cross and the necessity of self-denial and suffering is always a bitter pill for pleasure-seeking people to swallow. So often it requires a blind act of faith and trust in God to face a life-time of sacrifice of our own will. At the point of our meeting with Christ and God, we will always find the cross—a dying to self in order that we may rise to God. Like the rings of a tree, year by year, the struggle between ourselves and Christ's teaching results in a steady growth toward the union with God for which our hearts yearn. Some persons must follow the royal road of the cross throughout their life until the very moment of death; others, however, find that the way becomes more peaceful and happier as they progress in holiness. In one way or another, there will be a resurrection to a new and more glorious life than one ever believed possible.

At each new encounter with God, we experience new capabilities to understand, feel, and know the things of God. We still remain open to the values of earth; but now an additional aperture has been made between earth and heaven. Faith takes us through a gate into the City of God where we can make direct contact with the reality of God. We now see things of the earth through God's eyes; we see the beauty of God everywhere we look. We choose what is right and best by the power of God's will and we begin to comprehend God's truth. Our whole personality has been awakened by this meeting with Christ and God. All our capabilities for authenticity, transparency, solidarity, and encounter with our brethren on earth are greatly increased. We now know something of the fullness of the meaning of love—God's love—which is immensely greater than any possible human experience of love.

As a result of our encounters with God by faith, we begin to understand something of our true reality in the sight of God. We appreciate our significance before God; we know we are specially loved by our Creator. We mean something to God; we have meaning in his life. We are amazed to realize that God is actually pleased with us and enjoys our company and would miss us if we were not there.

We are not just a number in a vast indiscriminate mass of God's creation; rather we have been given a unique place in God's loving heart. "To those who conquer and prove victorious, I will give a white stone with a new name written on it, known only to him who receives it" (Rev. 2:17). This precious stone with our new name written on it is a symbol of that special place we have in God's heart once we conquer our pride and selfishness and give ourselves entirely to him.

As our surrender to these loving encounters with God continues, we will discover that our personality has become purified of egotism and converted into the likeness of Christ. Now we are able to bring together our whole nature into its true center, the inner self or person and in turn unite our human person to God's person. Our whole being becomes alert to God's least desires, to the needs of the community of mankind, and to the needs of our true inner nature. We have a true presentiment of what life will be like in the renewed creation of God's kingdom. We have been created for a dialogue of love with God and through God with all other persons in heaven and on earth. To the extent that we have made a total commitment of ourselves to God, to that degree can we experience a fulfillment of all our tasks upon earth.

> "Arise, my love, my dove, my beautiful one, make haste and come. For winter is now past, the rain is over and gone. The flowers have appeared on the earth, the time of pruning has come, the voice of the turtle dove is heard in our land, the fig tree has put forth its green figs, the vines in blossom have been giving forth fragrance. Arise, my love, my beautiful one and come."
>
> (Ct. 2:10-13)

185

BIBLIOGRAPHY

Assagioli, Roberto. *Psychosynthesis.* New York: Viking Press, 1965.

Berne, Eric. *Games People Play: The Psychology of Human Relationships.* New York: Grove Press, 1964.

Bornkamm, Gunther. *Jesus of Nazareth.* New York: Harper and Row, 1959.

Boylan, M. Eugene. *This Tremendous Lover.* Westminister, Maryland: The Newman Press, 1963.

Briggs, Katherine C. and Myers, Isabel Briggs. *Myers-Briggs Type Indicator Form G.* Palo Alto, California: Consulting Psychologists Press, Inc., 1957.

Brome, Vincent. *Jung, Man and Myth.* London: Granada Publishing, 1980.

Chauchard, Paul. *Teilhard de Chardin on Love and Suffering.* New York: Paulist, Deus Books, 1966.

Claremont de Castillejo, Irene. *Knowing Woman.* New York: Harper and Row, 1973.

Cuenot, Claude. *Teilhard de Chardin.* Baltimore: Helicon, 1965.

de Caussade, Jean-Pierre. *Abandonment to Divine Providence.* New York: Doubleday, Image Books, 1975.

Devaux, Andre A. *Teilhard and Womanhood.* New York: Paulist Press, Deus Books, 1968.

English, John J. *Choosing Life.* New York: Paulist Press, 1978.

—. *Spiritual Freedom.* Guelph, Ontario: Loyola House, 1977.

Erikson, Erik. *Gandhi's Truth.* New York: W. W. Norton, 1969.

—. *Identity: Youth and Crises.* New York: W. W. Norton, 1968.

—. *Insight and Responsibility.* New York: W. W. Norton, 1964.

Frankl, Viktor E. *Man's Search for Meaning.* New York: Pocket Books, 1963.

Fromm, Erich. *The Art of Loving.* New York: Bantam Books, 1963.

Goerres, Ida F. *The Hidden Face: A Study of St. Therese of Lisieux.* New York: Pantheon, 1959.

Goldbrunner, Josef. *Cure of Mind and Cure of Soul.* Notre Dame: University of Notre Dame Press, 1964.

—. *Holiness is Wholeness.* Notre Dame: University of Notre Dame Press, 1964.

—. *Individuation.* New York: Pantheon, 1956.

—. *Realization.* Notre Dame: University of Notre Dame Press, 1966.

Hall, Calvin and Nordby, Vernon. *A Primer of Jungian Psychology.* Bergenfield, New Jersey: The New American Library, 1973.

Hammarskjold, Dag. *Markings.* New York: Alfred A. Knopf, 1965.

Hannah, Barbara. *Jung: His Life and Work.* New York: G. P. Putnam's Sons, 1976.

Harding, M. Esther. *The Way of All Women.* New York: Harper and Row, 1970.

Jacobi, Jolande. *Complex, Archetype, Symbol: In the Psychology of C.G. Jung.* Princeton: Princeton University Press, 1959.

BIBLIOGRAPHY

Jaffe, Aniela. *The Myth of Meaning: Jung and the Expansion of Consciousness.* New York: Penguin Books, 1975.

Jung, Carl Gustav. *Aion.* Princeton: Princeton University Press, 1959.

—. *"Answer to Job", The Portable Jung.* New York: Viking Press, 1971.

—. *Man and His Symbols.* Garden City: Doubleday, 1964.

—. *Memories, Dreams, Reflections.* New York: Random House, 1965.

—. *Modern Man in Search of a Soul.* New York: Harcourt, Brace and World, 1933.

—. *Psychological Types.* Princeton: Princeton University Press, 1976.

—. *Psychology and Religion.* New Haven: Yale University Press, 1938.

—. *The Basic Writings of C. G. Jung.* New York: The Modern Library, 1959.

—. *The Psychology of the Transference.* Princeton: Princeton University Press, 1969.

—. *The Undiscovered Self.* Boston: Little, Brown and Company, 1957.

Keirsey, David and Bates, Marilyn. *Please Understand Me: An Essay On Temperament Styles.* Del Mar, California: Prometheus Nemesis Books, 1978.

Kelsey, Morton. *Encounter With God.* Minneapolis: Bethany Fellowship, 1972.

—. *Myth, History and Faith: The Remythologizing of Christianity.* New York: Paulist Press, 1974.

—. *The Other Side of Silence: A Guide to Christian Meditation.* New York: Paulist Press, 1976.

Kunkel, Fritz. *Creation Continues.* Waco, Texas: Word Books, 1973.

Lee, Harper. *To Kill A Mockingbird.* Philadelphia: Lippincott, 1960.

Lindbergh, Anne Morrow. *Gift From The Sea.* New York: Pantheon, 1955.

Luke, Helen M. *Dark Wood to White Rose: A Study of Meanings in Dante's Divine Comedy.* Pecos, New Mexico: Dove Publications, 1975.

Maslow, Abraham H. *Toward A Psychology of Being.* Princeton: D. Van Nostrand, 1962.

Menninger, Karl. *Whatever Became of Sin?* New York: Bantam Books, 1978.

Michael, Chester P. *A Christian Worldview.* Charlottesville, VA: The Open Door, Inc, 2002.

—. *A Comparison of the God-Talk of Thomas Aquinas and Charles Hartshorne.* Ann Arbor, Michigan: Zerox Microfilms, 1975.

—. *A New Day.* West Conshohocken, PA: Infinity Publishing, 2010.

—. *An Introduction to Spiritual Direction: A Psychological Approach for Directors and Directees.* New York: Paulist Press, 2004.

—. *Prayer and Temperament: Different Prayer Forms for Different Temperaments.* Charlottesville, VA: Open Door, 1984.

—. *The New Day of Christianity.* Baltimore: Helicon, 1965.

Peguy, Charles. *God Speaks.* New York: Pantheon, 1945.

BIBLIOGRAPHY

Perrin, Norman. *Rediscovering The Teachings of Jesus.* New York: Harper and Row, 1976.

Powell, John. *Why Am I Afraid To Love.* Niles, Illinois: Argus Communications, 1972.

Progoff, Ira. *Depth Psychology and Modern Man.* New York: McGraw-Hill, 1973.

Sanford, John A. *Dreams and Healing.* New York: Paulist Press, 1978.

___. *Healing and Wholeness.* New York: Paulist Press, 1977.

—. *The Invisible Partners.* New York: Paulist Press, 1980.

—. *The Kingdom Within.* Philadelphia: J. B. Lippincott, 1970.

Schwenck, Robert L. *Digging Deep: Penetrating Our Inner Selves Through Dream Symbols.* Pecos, New Mexico: Dove Publications, 1979.

Singer, June. *Boundaries of The Soul.* Garden City: Doubleday, 1973.

Sobrino, Jon. *Christology at the Crossroads.* Maryknoll, New York: Orbis Books, 1978.

Teilhard de Chardin, Pierre. *Building the Earth.* Denville, New Jersey: Dimension Books, 1965.

—. *Hymn of the Universe.* London: Collins, 1965.

—. *The Divine Milieu.* New York: Harper and Row, 1960.

—. *The Future of Man.* London: Collins, 1964.

Therese of Lisieux, St. *The Story of A Soul.* Washington: Institute of Carmelite Studies, 1972.

van der Post, Laurens. *Jung and The Story of Our Time.* New York: Random House, 1977.

van Kaam, Adrian. *Personality Fulfillment in the Spiritual Life.* Denville, New Jersey: Dimension Books, 1966.

Vann, Gerald. *The Heart of Man.* Garden City: Doubleday & Co., Image Books, 1960.

von Franz, Marie-Louise. *C. G. Jung: His Myth in Our Time.* Boston: Little, Brown and Company, 1975.

von Gagern, Frederick. *Difficulties in Married Life.* New York: Paulist Press, 1954.

Watkin, Dom Selred. *The Enemies of Love.* New York: Paulist Press, 1962.

White, Victor. *God and The Unconscious.* Cleveland: World Publishing Company, 1952.

—. *Soul and Psyche.* New York: Harper and Brothers, 1960.

Whitehead, Evelyn and James. *Christian Life Patterns.* Garden City, New York: Doubleday, 1979.

Whitmont, Edward. *The Symbolic Quest.* Princeton: Princeton University Press, 1969.

Wickes, Frances G. *The Inner World of Childhood.* New York: Appleton-Century-Crofts, 1927.

—. *The Inner World of Choice.* New York: Harper and Row, 1963.

—. *The Inner World of Man.* New York: Frederick Ungar Publishing Company, 1948.

INDEX

Made in the USA
Middletown, DE
04 September 2018